Envy—almost all of us struggle with it, and almost none of us will admit to it. In this eminently practical book, Tilly Dillehay shows us envy in its many disguises so that we can learn to recognize its itching and writhing presence in our own lives. More than that, she celebrates the goodness of borrowed glory in God's world, forcing us either to rot in our resentment or to learn to rejoice in the glorious inequalities that God so loves. This book is worth much reflection and meditation. I highly recommend it.

Joe Rigney, professor, Bethlehem College and Seminary, and author of *Lewis on the Christian Life* and *The Things of Earth*.

Seeing Green gently but persistently exposed the envy in my life and made me want something better. Tilly Dillehay writes honestly and compellingly about her own struggles and growth, leaving readers with confident hope that we don't have to give envy a home in our hearts.

Betsy Childs, editor, The Gospel Coalition, and author of *Seasons of Waiting*

Envy is a subtle and vicious sin, which usually aims at those closest to us—family, friends, neighbors, fellow workers, and church members. It is embarrassing to divulge, and thus it gnaws at our souls, filling us with rage at others' success or with satisfaction at their misfortune. Arguably, envy is the original sin that burned within Satan and has beset mankind throughout history. We see it in Scripture—from Cain to Saul to Joseph's brothers and to the Jews of Jesus's day who nailed him to a cross. In short, envy makes us unwitting accomplices of the devil, and it can destroy our souls. In her debut book, Tilly Dillehay helps us understand this sin in its various manifestations. With candid admission of her own struggle, penetrating insight into the human heart, and full confidence in God's mercy, Dillehay offers hope to those ensnared by this "green-eyed monster." She helps us see "borrowed glories" for what they are and fixes our gaze on the glories that await those "hidden with Christ in God" (Colossians 3:3). Read this book and serve your soul!

Ivan Mesa, editor, The Gospel Coalition

Tilly Dillehay has written a book which is both convicting and encouraging. Convicting because it names a sin which we all share but excuse as less important than others. Encouraging because it points the reader to the One who is owed all glory.

This book is full of Scripture as we face God's view of the sin of envy. We are shown the gospel that redeems us from all our sins. Christ is exalted and glorified. Women of all ages will benefit from reading Tilly Dillehay's book.

Caroline Newheiser, MA, certified counselor,
Association of Certified Biblical Counselors;
blogger, Biblical Counseling Coalition

Seeing Green

Tilly Dillehay

HARVEST HOUSE PUBLISHERS
EUGENE, OREGON

Cover by Darren Welch

Cover photo © maxim ibragimov / Shutterstock

Seeing Green
Copyright © 2018 Tilly Dillehay
Published by Harvest House Publishers
Eugene, Oregon 97408
www.harvesthousepublishers.com

ISBN 978-0-7369-7494-3 (pbk.)
ISBN 978-0-7369-7495-0 (eBook)

Library of Congress Cataloging-in-Publication Data

Names: Dillehay, Tilly, author.
Title: Seeing green / Tilly Dillehay.
Description: Eugene, Oregon : Harvest House Publishers, [2018]
Identifiers: LCCN 2018000559 (print) | LCCN 2018016426 (ebook) | ISBN
    9780736974950 (ebook) | ISBN 9780736974943 (pbk.)
Subjects: LCSH: Envy—Religious aspects—Christianity. | Joy—Religious
    aspects—Christianity.
Classification: LCC BV4627.E5 (ebook) | LCC BV4627.E5 D55 2018 (print) | DDC
    241/.3—dc23
LC record available at https://lccn.loc.gov/2018000559

Printed in the United States of America

18 19 20 21 22 23 24 25 26 / VP-SK / 10 9 8 7 6 5 4 3 2 1

To Sophie, Callie, Phoebe, and Emma, whose
borrowed glories turn my gaze upward in worship.

Contents

Foreword

The effect of reading *Seeing Green* by Tilly Dillehay is like that of a phenomenon I experience occasionally when I hear a word for the first time and then immediately notice it being used everywhere. Only in the case of *Seeing Green* it is not a word I suddenly notice. It's a ubiquitous virus in my heart that has stayed just under the radar of conviction. Suddenly I see envy everywhere in me. And no one likes catching a glimpse of the uglier dimensions of their heart.

We might describe a gifted author as one who can put words to convictions we have but cannot express. Or they describe with such clarity notions for which we cannot find words. But then there are those authors who make us see things we never knew existed. They have the ability to show us realities hidden in the wide-open of humanity. They see what others can't. They go about curing our collective blindness through words. Envy is not an easy thing to see. It is a harder thing to own. Tilly Dillehay accomplishes both.

To be confronted about an attitude is embarrassing. To have our ill tempers dragged into the open after we've gone to great lengths to disguise them is painful. Our first impulse is denial. We stand there like children with rocks in hand denying the existence of broken windows. Unwaveringly committed to an innocence that anyone with one good eye can see is false. Nothing is more disheartening about the human condition than its dedication to preserving its own dignity in the light of contrary facts. We would chew our arms off if it meant we could escape exposure.

Two versions of us are always in play—the one we want others to see and the one we keep out of sight. The latter is the true us. The amount of emotional energy we spend keeping our true selves under cover is extraordinary. Anyone shedding light on the real us creates shame, defensiveness, and panic. Exposure hurts.

What most people don't understand, however, is the freedom that exposure yields. It is contrary to our nature to stand in that light. But the freest person in the room is always the most exposed person in the room.

In the pages of this book you will find yourself doing something you would not normally do. You will drag yourself into the light. You will openly admit, if only to yourself at first, that beneath the apparent civility of your person lurks another. A person who struggles with envy. Believe me. You will see it. The reason this particular book will not send you scurrying for self-preserving cover is the self-deprecation of its author. Tilly's honesty is the glue that binds its pages together and the element that shaves down the edges of shame.

The brutal honesty with which she describes the darkness of her own heart is of an uncommon quality. People do not normally put themselves out there so thoroughly. But rather than unnerving us, it draws us in. It is such a rare species of honesty that we cannot help but admire it. She creates this safe space for us where we can finally admit without fear of rejection what we all already know about ourselves.

We finally say out loud what is the worst kept secret on the planet. Humanity is a tangled mess of discontent and unhappiness. Rather than counting our blessings, we mainly lust for the blessings of others. There, we said it. Thank you, Tilly, for breaking our silence.

What runs through the pages of this book is a barely perceptible exercise in self-awareness for the reader. An inadvertent but invaluable benefit is learning the skill of self-examination through Tilly's examination of her own heart. You don't even notice it's happening until it's over. She's our Mr. Miyagi of self-awareness.

"Wax on! Wax off!"

Most of us are lost somewhere in Johari's third window, unable to see about ourselves what is obvious to others. No one mentions the note that life has taped to our back listing all of our flaws for others to see. We cannot deal with what we don't know is there. We spend our lives roaming around a dark room tripping over the unseen obstacles of our own sinful nature and bad attitudes. We've no real idea why we do what we do and why we struggle so long from the same self-inflicted wounds. We've no real answer for why tension has always persisted in our relationships, or why our careers have tended to stay on the runway, or why a low-grade fever of unhappiness has gone unabated in our hearts. We continue to trip about in the dark.

In this book we behold the liberating effect of self-awareness. Tilly shows us what it is like to turn the light on and put everything in its place. We observe the very difficult, but very necessary, process of coming to terms with the things beneath the things of who we are. Every personal episode she shares is a play-by-play of the progression of self-awareness. The attention she pays to the subtleties of her own heart is such an important skill in the Christian practice of sanctification. We spend so much time repenting of the wrong things. The things that need to be admitted are much deeper than we care to admit. When we come out on the other side of this read, it's not only envy that we will have come to understand. It's our true hearts. This alone is worth the time spent in its pages.

What makes this work even more profound in my case is that I know the people involved. I am witness to the envy of which it speaks. I am pastor to the sisters Tilly so long resented. I know first-hand their skills, charisma, and giftedness. They are indeed enviable people. On more than one occasion, I sat in the same audience as Tilly, applauding and praising their performances. I have been an unashamed supporter of their careers. I have often referred to myself as their biggest fan. Until I read her confession, I had no idea that I had inadvertently been witness to a struggle.

This is why I received the honor of writing this foreword. The loop of confession is now closed, the exposure of her heart complete. Who else would ever think to ask the pastor of those we once resented to write a foreword for a book that chronicled the hurt of that season? Only a person who has nothing left to hide. Tilly's desire for honesty has no bounds. There is an evident integrity in such a request.

But I can also testify to the triumph of grace and the healing that has resulted. Tilly's family, especially the relationship between the siblings, is among the closest I have ever seen. Their relationship is a validation of everything she writes. Ironically, one might even say their relationship is enviable.

If you're holding this book in your hand reading this foreword, you are unintentionally admitting you have a problem with envy. Why else would anyone read a book on envy? Or you suspect envy might be related to some issues in your life and want to know for sure. Or you think you are the exception and want to test your character against its contents.

If you are the first category of reader, welcome. You are not alone.

You can expect to find clarity, wisdom, encouragement, and biblical guidance on how to subdue the envy that has dogged your life. If you are the second category of reader, your suspicions will be confirmed momentarily. Welcome. You will find clarity, wisdom, encouragement, and biblical guidance on how to subdue the envy you hoped wasn't there. If you are the third category of reader, you are not the exception. Welcome. You will find clarity, wisdom, encouragement, and biblical guidance on how to subdue the envy you had no idea existed.

No one gets out of this book unscathed. No one escapes. We all suffer from the vile tendency to envy the lives of others. Even people who have everything anyone could ever want envy what others have. Envy transcends station and status. It is a universal blight. Go ahead and join the rest of us in admitting defeat. Take up this book and read it in the presence of all. No one will be surprised, and you will be all the more blessed by doing so.

Byron Yawn
Author of *What Every Man Wishes His Father Had Told Him* and pastor of Community Bible Church, Nashville, Tennessee

When the Music Hurts

It was a bitter night, I remember; there was a sleeve of frost around the glass door of the coffee shop. I was a sophomore in college, and I still thought I wanted to be a jazz singer.

My self-released CD of cover tunes had been sold online and to friends and family members; that tiny first printing was nearly gone. It had been little or no trouble to me to make the album and no work to speak of, and it had done nothing to teach me about music theory or how to be onstage.

It had also done nothing to dampen my daydreams of being the ingénue jazz singer, bringing old blues into a new era, making the old style fresh and smart and young. In these dreams, the public acknowledged my beauty, voice, and brains in exactly equal measure. The kids in my youth group were embarrassed about not talking to me much. Old enemies dropped my name at school and work, offhandedly mentioning that they knew Tilly Cryar personally.

But on this particular cold night, I wasn't daydreaming.

I walked into the coffee shop alone; some of my family members were already there. Two of my sisters were in the back, the older one ordering something. The other two—the ones just younger than me—were standing nervously in a corner where the microphones had been set up. They shifted their eyes around; they laughed in little spurts at their friends who had come to see them. They fiddled around with the instrument cases even though everything was ready.

At seven o'clock, an employee of the coffee shop must have given some kind of green light because the girls stepped behind the microphones. Their shaking hands strapped on a ukulele, a guitar. They began the first chord progression; I don't remember if back then only one kept rhythm or if both of them did, or if they had already begun to use those wonderful finger-picking patterns.

But the song was one they had written themselves. Callie, the older, opened her mouth and began to sing, and her voice made us all stop what we were doing. Phoebe, the younger, began to harmonize. It was a sweet, soulful song. The lyrics were like precious stones, one line after another—not polished yet, a little bumpy, but the richness was all there.

These two girls were just teenagers. Before now, they'd refused to play their songs even for the family. They'd taken Papa's eight-track recorder and secreted away into their rooms, writing and recording clips, afraid at first even to show things to each other.

And even that night onstage, they were no good at all at talking to the crowd. Self-conscious and abrupt between songs, they moved from one tune to the next as quickly as possible. But no one minded. The brilliance was there; it was shimmering through the room. My younger sisters had incubated something in secret, without my knowing anything about it—and now I was a witness for the first time.

I don't know if it was the sweetness in the music or the wisdom in the lyrics that made me cry, sitting at a table in the back.

It might have been the envy.

Because whatever else I felt, whatever sisterly joy or swell of exuberance that good art produces, there was envy with it. I could hardly bear the sting of glory I was seeing. Glory can be magnetic, but glory—especially if it's a glory you've wanted for yourself—can also be terrible.

After that night, the girls kept working. They cultivated their musical instinct until it became real discipline. They formed a band. They wrote and wrote and wrote. They recorded an album; they hired a booking agent. They struggled into doing other coffee shop gigs and bought a horrible van that broke down on them repeatedly.

As the years progressed—and it has been years of working and crafting their way through what is still a booming American folk music scene—I found that I could not bear the music anymore. I was all right hearing my sisters praised by friends or family or even strangers. In those cases, I could smile and nod and agree…but going to their concerts was torture.

In the privacy of a dark church or auditorium, sitting and listening to the art that had risen and flowered so close to me was a painful experience. When I was listening, when another song was unveiled, when another vocal styling was presented, when I saw yet again that stage presence had improved with practice and their songwriting had tuned itself further—I couldn't pretend the glory away.

Years went by. The envy in my heart—unacknowledged, never even whispered to myself or to a closest friend—lived on for years. Fueled by the hatred of glory that I wanted for myself, I began to avoid the music. I avoided talking about it. I avoided hearing it. I politely took home each record as it came, listened to it once, and buried it in a drawer or closet. I found myself unable to naturally and easily discuss my sisters' current work with them, so I simply didn't.

That kind of silence couldn't have gone unnoticed. They probably assumed I thought they weren't any good or that I was simply apathetic…or too busy and self-absorbed to pay attention.

Years of supportive language have been lost, never to return. My envy ate up years of friendship with the playmates of my youth, and damage was undoubtedly done. Repentance and restoration has come only through open apologies, helped along by adulthood, marriage, and children. My sisters and I know and love each other again.

But even when I look plainly at the losses incurred through the sin of envy and mourn them, it's hard to imagine those years any other way. What could have been more natural than my reaction? How could I have felt differently? Could I have ceased caring about music? Stopped wanting to be a musician? Quit wishing that I could sing my own music and hear that kind of applause? It's true that I didn't really want to be a musician myself—I'd already found out that I was unwilling to do the work and face the rejection of slogging into it. But could I really have prevented that gut reaction of horror when I saw two people so close to myself looking so glorious and accomplishing exactly what I hadn't accomplished? Being exactly what I had wanted to be? *Who*—I asked myself, when the word *envy* did eventually suggest itself a few years later—*could have possibly reacted any differently?*

In a way, I was right. There's nothing more natural than envy: it belongs to the debased mind of a *natural* man, not to a mind that has been transformed *supernaturally* by the Holy Spirit (Romans 1:28-31; James 3:14-16).

Envy is absolutely understandable. Everybody gets it when we read a story and one of the characters (usually the bad guy, or at best a ruefully flawed protagonist) is eaten up with envy. Though ugly and generally not admired or explicitly named, envy is depicted constantly in popular culture. If you've ever watched a reality show or read Shakespeare or heard the song "Girl Next Door" by Saving Jane, you know what envy smells like.

And if you're like most of the natural men and women walking around this planet in a fleshly suit, you probably know what envy feels like too.

This book is for you. It is written for Christians. It is to be used in the battle—the fighting and killing of envy.

To get at the envy in the first place, we need to see it more clearly. So we are going to look at its deepest heart-level motivations. To do that, we're going to have a discussion about borrowed glory and the inequality of glory portions that each of us has received from the Father. We'll take a walk through seven different types of glory that especially seem to inspire envy in human hearts. And in the end, we will follow the glory to its source. We'll find that doing battle against envy involves faith in and worship of God's superior and essential glory.

The goal of this book is to help us all battle envy by changing the way we see. What if, instead of envying those whom we perceive to be superior to us in whatever way we happen to value, we began to look upon them as part of the Great Story—players in God's theater, prisms reflecting aspects of God's glory that we might never see in ourselves? Might we not learn greater contentment? Might we not learn to rejoice with those who rejoice? To love our neighbor as ourselves? God help us, we might. The Holy Spirit is on our side.

1

What Is Glory?
And What Does Envy
Have to Do with It?

*That cushiony moss, that coldness and sound and dancing light
were no doubt very minor blessings compared with "the means
of grace and the hope of glory." But then they were manifest...
They were not the hope of glory, they were an exposition of the
glory itself...I was learning the far more secret doctrine that
pleasures are shafts of the glory as it strikes our [senses].*

C.S. LEWIS, *Letters to Malcolm*

Once, when I was a teenager, I saw Nicole Kidman and her husband, Keith Urban, at the movie theater.

My friend and I were walking down a brick hallway headed into the theater entrance, and she and Keith were walking toward us. I instantly knew it was her. I felt a surge of blood in my fingertips and my face became hot, as if I were embarrassed. I stared, I tried not to stare, I successfully looked away, and then, as they walked past me within just a few feet, I stared again.

She was tall. They were laughing.

My friend and I turned to each other after passing them.

"Was that...?"

"Yes, it *was*."

And without even communicating, we turned around and

followed them, just to get close to them again. We followed them to the curb where they were waiting with the self-satisfied theater security person who had been escorting them. They were waiting for their car, I guess. We walked right out into the parking lot, pretending again that we didn't see them. As we went, somebody else stopped and asked for an autograph.

We'd never have done that. We were much too cool.

My friend and I just kept walking, all the way to our car, and then got in, forgetting about the movie we had come to see. Both of us found that we were shaking—actually shaking. And for the rest of the night, I had a euphoric sense of promise, as if something big was about to change my life forever. I had a dizzy, infatuated image of Nicole's hair from up close.

We were full of adrenaline because we'd had an encounter with a movie star and her country music star husband.

Just a couple of dumb teenagers acting out a private drama, we were illustrating something about human nature that I didn't understand until much later.

Something is wrong with us. Something is missing. We've been locked out of something, and we want more than anything else to be let back in. Something is calling to us. We want to be enveloped by it, whatever it is. So when we find an experience that lets us brush our fingers, even for a moment, on this beauty or truth or fame or love that seems to lurk behind the locked doors of the world around us, we will do whatever it takes to chase that experience down for another taste.

I'm going to call this *something* by a shorthand word. Glory.

The Glory of God

My encounter with a shimmering, glowing star in the cinema firmament was similar, in a pathetic way, to other encounters that people have had with glory.

In Exodus, we read about the way that the Israelites reacted to Moses. Not to God himself but to Moses—because Moses had gotten close to where God was and had gotten glory all over himself.

Moses came down from Mount Sinai with new stone copies of the Ten Commandments. He was unaware that "the skin of his face shone because he had been talking with God" (Exodus 34:29). But the people were immediately aware. They felt a surge of adrenaline as it hit them: *He's glowing.* They were terrified, and no one would even come near him.

Eventually, Moses called to them, his brother and the other leaders came over, and he talked with them. He had been up on the mountain for 40 days and 40 nights without food or drink, sustained by God himself. The shining didn't stop, so Moses ended up having to put a veil over his face, which he wore whenever he came out from speaking to God.

This was just secondhand glory, and it was still too much for the people to bear. The glowing face of Moses was only a physical metaphor for a spiritual reality: *You can't get too close to glory without it affecting you.*

In Paul's second letter to the Corinthians, he discussed this veil over Moses's face and marveled at the fact that the glory of law, which is a dying glory, had been so far surpassed by the glory of Christ. Yet Christ is even now making men and women of glory who are capable of withstanding and engaging his glory unveiled!

> Since we have such a hope, we are very bold, not like Moses, who would put a veil over his face so that the Israelites might not gaze at the outcome of what was being brought to an end. But their minds were hardened. For to this day, when they read the old covenant, that same veil remains unlifted, because only through Christ is it taken away. Yes, to this day whenever Moses is read a

> veil lies over their hearts. But when one turns to the
> Lord, the veil is removed. Now the Lord is the Spirit, and
> where the Spirit of the Lord is, there is freedom. And we
> all, with unveiled face, beholding the glory of the Lord,
> are being transformed into the same image from one
> degree of glory to another. For this comes from the Lord
> who is the Spirit (2 Corinthians 3:12-18).

What does that mean? What is God's glory, according to the
Bible?

The glory of God can be described with a range of terms. It is his
brightness, his splendor, and his radiance. It is his weightiness, his
power, and his majesty. It is his fame, his honor, and his renown. In
the words of Douglas Moo, "'Glory' signifies the splendor and majesty that belong intrinsically to the one true God."[1]

Note the word *intrinsically*. Glory is something God possesses
by his very nature. He can't not have it. His glory doesn't depend
upon human or angelic recognition. *If the glory of God shone forth
and nobody saw it, would he still be glorious?* The answer is yes. On
the other hand, since God is triune in his nature, there is also a real
sense in which the glory of God has never been totally unseen or
unadored, even before the universe was made (John 17:5).

So God's glory is the weight, splendor, and majesty that he possessed by his very nature before anything else ever existed. Yet when
the Bible speaks of God's glory, it usually refers to his glory as it
shines forth in history—as it is displayed and reflected in his mighty
acts of creation and redemption.

Though he was neither lonely nor discontented, nevertheless, in
the overflow of his generosity, God created the universe as a theater
for his glory. The heavens declare it. The earth is filled with it. So if
we fail to see it, then we must be blind.

Do you recognize glory in the world around you? *Glory*, for

Christians, can be a rather ephemeral word. It may not have come home to roost in your everyday understanding yet. For many people, *glory* evokes only vague, bland ideas about God's being very big or very shiny. Another definition would be only partially useful right now. For some things, lists and stories are better than definitions. Let me make a list for you of ways that glory can be understood:

- God is the reason that every good thing you experience reminds you of some other good experience that is lost in either the past or in the future. *Nostalgia hints at glory.*

- God is the reason that when you fall in love, you feel like every good thing in you is being called out and forward and up. *Love hints at glory.*

- God is the reason that you still remember the day your sixth-grade teacher told you your paper was "Excellent! You really grasped the material!" God is also the reason that you have spent your entire life trying to get your father to say similar words. *Proper praise from a superior hints at glory.*

- God is the reason that you've always longed to go to Paris, and he is the reason that when you make it to Paris you long even more to get back home. *Yearning for another land hints at glory.*

- God is the reason that music moves you as it does, stories swell your soul, and you could easily spend all your weekends gazing at paintings or photography or pretty dresses. *Art hints at glory.*

- God is even the reason that you hate to be cut out of cliques and why there are people who spend their entire lives social climbing. *The desire to be "inside" hints at glory.*

God's glory is what we will be living in the presence and enjoyment of for all eternity. It is all things meaningful, all things worthwhile, all things beautiful, and all things that quicken the pulse with joy and quicken the mind with sight.

You may not have connected your wanderlust to see Asia with the promises in Scripture that you will "depart and be with Christ" (Philippians 1:23), but the desires are tied. You may never have connected your relentless pursuit of approval from your boss with the promise that in Christ, you'll hear, "Well done, good and faithful servant" (Matthew 25:23), but these desires are intimately related.

You also may never have noticed that "enter into the joy of your master" is one of the next statements in that verse. It's as if joy were the most natural way in the world to describe both God's state and our state in his presence. And what is it that people are always saying to describe an experience or sight or personal interaction? "It made me happy." It brought you joy; what else do I need to know about the concert or the movie or your visit with cousin Ted? And these joys that we have already tasted are only a nibble next to the feast, a Zippo next to the sun of joy we will experience in the presence of God's glory.

So glory is the shining joy, beauty, intelligence, power, and goodness of God himself. It compels all who see it to respond in either worship or loathing.

Man, the Glory Mirror

Man was created to worship God's glory, and we saw in that earlier list of experiences that our appetite for God's glory is one of the most foundational motives in our lives. We have longings. It's one of the things that sets us apart from the animals.

But here's another thing that sets us apart from the animals. I'm going to call this thing *borrowed glory*. So now I've got another term to straighten out. What do I mean by *borrowed glory*?

Man, according to the order of creation detailed in Genesis 1 and 2, is God's crowning creation. If we are naming the things God made that shine his glory forth most spectacularly, there are all kinds of things competing for the list: the Grand Canyon, those mysterious sea creatures living along the Mariana Trench, a butterfly's wings, or the Salar de Uyuni, the huge salt flat in Bolivia. But according to the climactic order of the creation account, none of those things was God's crowning creation. That distinction is reserved for mankind.

We are the only created beings ever said to be made in God's own image. Not even the angels can boast that. We were, in a unique sense, "crowned…with glory and honor" (Psalm 8:5). This glory is a borrowed glory, a reflected glory. The glory of the moon rather than the glory of the sun. But it is a real glory nonetheless.

What does it mean to say that man possesses *borrowed glory*?

Let me answer this question with another question. Have you ever encountered a person and then described them to someone else later as *intimidating*? What about *fascinating*? *Inspiring*? I am sure you've met an older person or a friend of the same gender or a peer of the opposite gender who instantly dazzled you. Surely you have been rendered jittery and awkward in some specific person's presence, and not because you were romantically attracted to him or her. Surely you have also been rendered serene and happy in someone's presence.

What is it about these people that gives them such power over you? Why is it that we can all guess what you mean when you say, "She was intimidating"?

And what relationship, if any, does this have to the glory of God? Would we use the word *intimidating* to describe God? I don't think so—not exactly. We wouldn't apply this word to our relationship with God because it would be a gross understatement. We won't be intimidated when we finally stand before the God of heaven, any more than we will be *amused* or *fascinated*.

No. We will be devastated, overwhelmed, terrified, enamored, and silenced. We will find that our entire previous existence is both done away with and justified, both crushed and consummated.

That is what the glory of God means. *Intimidated* doesn't begin to describe it.

But having established that, we should acknowledge something else. Those words we use to describe people, such as *intimidating, fascinating, inspiring,* and *infatuating,* are like the younger cousins of words we use to describe God. When we say we are intimidated by a person, this is like a miniature version of the awe or reverence that we feel toward the God in whose image they are made.

These things are related. The relationship is derivative, metaphorical. One glory is borrowed from the other and was made to whisper things about the other.

And because it was borrowed from the One for whom all glory was named, there is something very real and unavoidable about the glory of human beings. We are terrible and lovely creations, purposeful and intelligent and attractive (though while under the curse of sin, also willful and insane and hideous).

When you see a truly beautiful woman on the street, it is hard to pretend she isn't there. Beauty demands a response, whether it's admiration or hatred or desire. When you listen to a skilled politician craft his words for a crowd, you can almost feel the weight of his influence. Excellent communication demands a response. When you talk to a true artist about his work, the power of his vision and talent thrums like an engine beneath the conversation. Good art demands a response.

Glory is always like that. It demands response.

Even in tiny amounts. Even the broken shards of glory that you see in a fallen human. You were made to respond.

But as real as the glories of man feel, they are only real because of where they came from. And the fact that they are borrowed means that they're only ours for a lifetime. Every person, even an enemy of God, gets to wear some kind of borrowed glory, because even the enemies of God are made in his image.

"What is man that you are mindful of him, and the son of man that you care for him?" asks the psalmist. "Yet…[you have] crowned him with glory and honor…O Lord, our Lord, how majestic is your name in all the earth" (Psalm 8).

Cut Off from the Source

Our appetite for glory has been insatiable and unsatiated ever since one important event in history.

Before the Fall, man drank fully of God's glory in an everyday setting. They walked with him the way you would go on an afternoon stroll with a friend. They heard his voice—a voice that must have been etched in their memories for the rest of their lives, the way your mother's is in yours. They watched his facial expressions. They heard the original botanist's commentary on what he had recently made. And they were more than able to enjoy these things because of their own state, possessing the maximum worshipful potential of creatures made in God's own image. They were unspoiled mirrors, shining without self-consciousness the glory of their Father.

One day, a serpent who had already reached for an improper glory and destroyed himself showed up in the garden. John Milton described what he imagines to be Satan's frame of mind in *Paradise Lost*. Satan was talking to a fellow rebel, marveling at the way his formerly glorious comrade had changed since the rebellion. Then, still unrepentant, he concluded:

All is not lost—the unconquerable will,
And study of revenge, immortal hate,
And courage never to submit or yield...
That glory never shall his wrath or might
Extort from me. To bow and sue for grace...
That were an ignominy and shame beneath
This downfall.[2]

In other words, Satan recognized the loss of one kind of glory, but he concluded that he'd prefer the twisted glory of never submitting or yielding, of revenge and immortal hatred. This was preferable to submission, in his mind. Later he spoke the famous line, "Better to reign in Hell than serve in Heaven."[3]

Christian tradition has it that Satan was motivated by envy and revenge when he came to tempt the woman. Milton certainly interpreted it this way. He could not bear to see their unspoiled and unique brand of glory—in the image of the Father, remember—and he was driven to destroy it. He told his army in a war council:

Though Heaven be shut,
And Heaven's high Arbitrator sit secure
In his own strength, this place [Earth] may lie exposed,
...here, perhaps,
Some advantageous act may be achieved...
To waste his whole creation, or possess
All as our own, and drive, as we were driven,
The puny habitants; or, if not drive,
Seduce them to our party, that their God
May prove their foe.[4]

This is exactly what Satan accomplished. In the garden, Eve chose desire over obedience. She considered equality with God a thing to be grasped, instead of glorying in the position she was created to fill. Her husband followed, and everything changed in a moment.

God, coming to find the cringing, hiding pair, told them that they would now experience pain previously unknown to them, that they would be thwarted in their endeavors and desires, and that their glorious relationships would be marred (Genesis 3:16-19). Underscoring the change, he made clothing for them to cover bodies that were once gloriously unashamed and healthy, undying and innocent. Then, in a stroke that was perhaps more unbearable than any other, God sent them out of the only home they'd known...*and away from his presence.*

They had fallen short of the source of the glory. Having rejected the source of the glory on his terms, they were cursed, doomed to generations of glory-hunger.

We have all been cut off from the source of the glory (although Christians live under this separation in a different way). Glory is now a commodity, scarce. Scarcity inflates the value of the glory. Sin and suffering have marred our ability to reflect the light, and like cracked and mottled mirrors, we only dimly remind ourselves and each other of the glory for which we hunger.

But even this dim reminder is powerful among such hungry people.

Without access to the source of the real glory, we go nuts over any little thing that reminds us of it. The personal glories each person has been gifted with—their beauties, their personalities, their creations, their physical talents, their money, their ability to love others—we watch and compare and adore and attack these glories wherever we find them.

But even this borrowed glory is somewhat ephemeral. People want different kinds of it, and people see it in different ways. I may care a whole lot about the glorious musical talent of my sisters, but someone else would be much more impressed by stand-up comedy. I may not be intimidated by one friend's ability to make money, but her ability to make people like her might turn me green. One girl falls in love with a man because he is a country boy; another falls in love with someone for *not* being a country boy.

It's as if we're trying to work with a new kind of currency—shiny beads of glory in different colors. Everyone wants a handful, but the standards of measurement are confused because there are no dollar amounts stamped on bills. We're not sure whether two units of beauty are worth one unit of brains; we're not sure if one unit of charisma trumps the money card.

We just know that there is glory and that sometimes the individuals around us possess it in uncomfortable amounts. This brings us to our next problem: What happens when you come face-to-face with a person who has more of the borrowed glory than you have? What if it's the kind of glory that you *most especially wanted for yourself*?

Discussion Questions

- In what ways does the list on page 19 paint a picture for you of the word *glory*? What are some other experiences you've had that have stuck with you, that you associate with longing or joy?

- Describe some characteristics you've noticed in people that blew you away (attributes that anyone could have, not just Christians).

- What are some reactions you've had to these people (excitement, intimidation, admiration, envy, etc.)?

2

The Unbearable Inequality: Understanding Envy

Envy is the art of counting the other fellow's blessings instead of your own.

HAROLD G. COFFIN

For anyone who is preoccupied with fairness, the inequality of the world is downright unbearable. Why God allows inequality to exist in the first place is hard to understand, but he allows it. Sometimes it seems that he even condones it or creates it himself.

This just rubs us in all the wrong ways.

How could the Lord of all creation say things like, "To you it has been given to know the secrets of the kingdom of heaven, but to them it has not been given. For to the one who has, more will be given, and he will have an abundance, but from the one who has not, even what he has will be taken away" (Matthew 13:11-12)?

What?

What did Jesus mean, those who have will get more? What did he mean, those who are lacking will have even that little portion taken away? That system is not what I would have chosen if I were doing the choosing.

Inequality clearly abounds in the spiritual world, so is it surprising to find inequality in the temporal world too? Look around you: The glory is distributed like paint in textured, uneven swaths across God's creation. One person has a huge dab of brains. Another has a great, big, fat stripe of beauty. Another person has swirls of money, creative talent, *and* interpersonal skill.

What's fair about this? In our way of thinking, fairness is assumed to be the highest value. Our culture rages against inequality as undemocratic and oppressive. Alternately, we are called on to pretend the inequality doesn't exist or to do whatever it takes to flatten the inequality out of existence.

If you walk into a school system and dare to imply that Johnny may be naturally smarter than Bobby, or that Jane is objectively prettier than Maddie, then you'll get shouted down. Smarter? *No, Johnny only makes higher grades because has enjoyed certain advantages that Bobby has not. Let's change the grading system again!* Prettier? *How dare you suggest that these girls are not equally beautiful in their own way!*

It burns the ears of the average person to acknowledge that some people are born with natural abilities that others are born without. We want to believe everyone has the chance to be somebody someday. That's the American dream. Maybe you were born poor or plain or with only one parent still hanging around, or maybe you were raised in such a way that it's hard for you to play nice with other people. The idea is that everybody has the opportunity to clamber their way to the top. No matter their beginnings, they should be able to end up as well as anyone else.

It just kills us to know, deep down, that this isn't really true. People aren't born with the same ingenuity. They aren't born with the same willingness to work hard. Not everybody is able to make people like them, and not everybody is born with the same intelligence or given the same opportunity to hone it. If we weren't so preoccu-pied with the fairness value system, we would admit what we already know. Life's not fair. Kids in an elementary school classroom know this. Instinctively, they understand that some kids have more or know more or love more or do more than others.

The world isn't fair. The glory isn't handed out like ration packs, with everybody getting 100 grams a week.

It's this basic outrage about portion size that we need to address here. Surely, if God is a good God and a just God, then there must be a way to understand the system. Is it simply that this world is not our home and everything is going to be leveled out in the end? In a way, yes. But also in a way, everything is going to be finally sorted in the end. Not only will everybody not end up with the same portion, but the great divide between people will be widened and finalized. Some will get everything, and others will get nothing. Some will be finally approved, and others will be finally disapproved.

I'm writing as much to try to reconcile my own heart to this as to reconcile anyone else's. If I dislike inequality at the relatively incon-sequential level (in things like money and looks), then I absolutely hate inequality at the eternal and essential level.

I don't want to think that there is such a thing as a sheep and a goat (Matthew 25:31-36). I don't want to think that there is such a thing as a wheat plant and a weed (Matthew 13:24-30). I really hate to think that there are virgins who remember their oil and virgins who forget their oil (Matthew 25:1-13), and I hate that somebody is not going into the wedding feast because they didn't dress them-selves properly (Matthew 22:1-14).

But if Jesus said it, then I have to try to understand it. My heart is the thing that must change, break, and be reformed to recognize and love the system. I don't have the right or the strength to "kick against the goads" (Acts 26:14).

Envy, Defined

"A tranquil heart gives life to the flesh," says Proverbs 14:30, "but makes the bones rot." This is the perfect picture of the gangrenous pain we experience when we give ourselves up to envy. Shakespeare called it the "green sickness" and the "green-eyed monster."[2]

Paul diagnosed the whole human race in Romans 1:28-31:

> Since they did not see fit to acknowledge God, God gave them up to a debased mind...they are full of envy, murder, strife, deceit, maliciousness. They are gossips, slanderers, haters of God, insolent, haughty, boastful, inventors of evil, disobedient to parents, foolish, faithless, heartless, ruthless.

As you can see, envy begins the list of sins that fill the heart of man, but several of the items listed after envy typically come with the envy package. Strife, deceit, maliciousness, gossip, slander, and boasting often come as symptoms or siblings of envy.

Paul was saying that these are among the worst blights on mankind; this is what it looks like for us to be given up "to a debased mind." These are the symptoms of refusing to acknowledge God, and they are ugly.

Yes, envy is very ugly. I never said it wasn't.

Here is a good, basic definition of *envy*:

> Envy is an emotion that is essentially both selfish and malevolent. It is aimed at persons, and implies dislike of the one who possesses what the envious man himself covets or desires, and a wish to harm him. Graspingness for self and ill-will lie at the basis of it. There is in it also a consciousness of inferiority to the person envied, and a chafing under this consciousness. He who has got

what I envy is felt by me to have the advantage of me, and I resent it.[1]

Many scholars throughout history have also had something to say about envy, and they are all pretty much agreed on what it means.

- "Envy is pain at the sight of [others'] good fortune" (Aristotle).[2]

- "[Envy is] sorrow for another's good" (Thomas Aquinas).[3]

- "[Envy is] dissatisfaction with our place in God's order of creation, manifested in begrudging his gifts to others" (Augustine).[4]

- "Envy is a spirit of opposition to [the] happiness [of others]…compared with [our] own" (Jonathan Edwards).[5]

- "[Envy is] the grudging spirit that cannot bear to contemplate someone else's prosperity" (F.F. Bruce).[6]

- "[Envy is] the consuming desire to have everybody else as unsuccessful as you are" (Frederick Buechner).[7]

- "Envy is a feeling of unhappiness at the blessing and fortune of others" (Joe Rigney).[8]

Envy is different from covetousness and jealousy. This is a simple issue of semantics. People often say *jealous* when what they mean is *envious*. While there is some overlap between these two words, as well as the word *covetous*, here is a basic way to differentiate.

Jealousy is a feeling of discomfort and anger that something you have is being threatened. This means that jealousy can sometimes be righteous. God himself is a jealous God (Exodus 20:5-6; Deuteronomy 6:15). Envy, in contrast, is distress over something that *someone else* possesses. It is always sinful, and it is not a feeling ever attributed to God.[9]

Covetousness is the desire for what someone else possesses. It would be satisfied simply to have what the other person has. Envy, in contrast, takes it personally that the other person has what he has, and would be satisfied to see the possession or quality destroyed rather than see the other person enjoying it.

Envy Thrives Among Peers

We will not be talking about envying the lifestyles of the rich and famous in this book. The brand of envy we are dealing with is more of a backyard envy, born and bred at home. It's the kind of envy that interrupts brotherly love and wreaks havoc on fellowship in the church. Envy in the pews and at the office and between friends.

This is the kind of malice Paul talked about in his laundry list of sins that plague the natural man. It's hard to feel this kind of malice for someone you've never met. The other person needs to be close enough to you that you feel a rivalry with him or her.

Jesus knew this. "A prophet is not without honor," he observed once, "except in his hometown and among his relatives and in his own household" (Mark 6:4). He recognized that glory burns more when it is close enough to touch you. He knew that when you've watched a person grow up from diapers, you'll have a hard time accepting his power when he comes into it.

Another strange thing about envy: People usually envy things they already have in some measure. If you've been called smart, you're more likely to envy genius. If you've got a car, you're more likely to want a nicer car than another man who has no car at all. A pretty woman is usually more envious of a beautiful woman than a plain-looking woman.

A dog would never have grasped for God's power and knowledge the way Satan and Eve did. Nor could it have. It was precisely Satan and Eve's borrowed glory that made them capable of recognizing glory, valuing it, and ultimately, falling over it.

Envy Comes with a Feeling of Inferiority

In *Screwtape Proposes a Toast,* C.S. Lewis writes about the relationship between inferiority and envy:

> No man who says *I'm as good as you* believes it. He would not say it if he did. The St. Bernard never says it to the toy dog, nor the scholar to the dunce, nor the employable to the bum, nor the pretty woman to the plain. The claim to equality, outside the strictly political field, is made only by those who feel themselves to be in some way inferior. What it expresses is precisely the itching, smarting, writhing awareness of inferiority which the patient refuses to accept.[10]

This *writhing, itching awareness* is at the heart of envy. The inferiority is sometimes only a felt inferiority on the part of the envier, but in all cases, a sense of inferiority is there. And it hurts, as Screwtape would say, like hell.

Envy Is Destructive Rather Than Motivational

Strange thing: envy is more interested in getting rid of the other person's advantage than in acquiring it for itself. In a complete, demonic reverse of logic, the envious person believes that it would be better for no one to have it than for another person to have it while he himself goes without.

Think of the two women who came to Solomon with one live baby and one dead baby (1 Kings 3:16-28). They both claimed the live one was theirs, that the other woman had rolled over her baby in the middle of the night and killed it. Solomon's job was to figure out which woman was telling the truth, and in the end, he relied on a basic understanding of envy to tell him. He ordered the live baby cut in half and given to both women.

The first woman said, "All right; so be it. Kill the kid."

The second said, "No! No, let this woman have the baby; only let it live."

Solomon understood the human heart. He knew that a true mother would jump to stop the barbarism because she would do anything to save her baby's life, including giving it up to her lying friend. More importantly, he knew that an envious woman, the kind who would stoop to lying about whose baby is whose, would be tripped up by her own sin. And she was. She gave in to the lowest impulse of envy—the destructive, murderous one—preferring to see a baby dead than to see a live baby in someone else's arms. This is how she showed her hand. Solomon knew that she had no love for the child and wasn't, in fact, the true mother.

Envy does not generally motivate us to better ourselves. It motivates us to destroy others.

There's a good joke illustrating this:

> Once there was an Englishman, a Frenchman, and a Russian walking along the beach. They found a genie's bottle and rubbed it, and were each granted a wish.
>
> The Englishman said, "Well, my neighbor has a beautiful house, the most beautiful house in our neighborhood, with climbing roses and pillars and four big bedrooms. I want a house like that, but maybe with a little extra room in the kitchen and a larger backyard."
>
> "Done," said the genie.
>
> The Frenchman said, "All right, my neighbor has a wife who is just absolutely gorgeous. She is also very sweet,

cooks great meals, compliments him all the time, and lets him go golfing on the weekends. I want a wife like that, but blonde instead of brunette, and who also has some money in the bank that we can live off of."

"Done," said the genie.

The Russian said, "My neighbor has a cow. It gives the richest, creamiest milk in a hundred miles. Everybody comes from far and wide to taste this cow's milk, and she gives gallons of it every day. I want that cow…dead!"

The Tennessee Walker

There is a man in my county who walks all day long.

He has matted blonde and silver hair that hangs down below his ears and a beard the same color that hangs over his chest. From spring until fall, he wears a short-sleeve, button-down shirt, which he keeps unbuttoned. There is a strip of his stomach about six inches wide that is tanned a deep brown, but when you get close to him and his shirt gapes a little, you can see that the rest of his front is still pale. Some mornings, he carries a tin coffee mug.

He lives about a mile from the house I used to live in, in a rural area on a deserted road. He walks from early in the morning until the sun goes down. But he never leaves the road in front of his house. Instead of walking up the road or down the road, he walks *across* it.

The same ten paces. Over and over again, back and forth, he goes across the road and back, across the road and back. Miles and miles, day in and day out, in all kinds of weather.

No one knows why he does it.

People say his brain was damaged by acid. Some say he took drugs in the 1970s, and others say that when he was a boy somebody snuck actual acid into his milk at school as a joke and it messed him up. Others have told me that he has post-traumatic stress disorder from fighting in a war. Nobody really knows, it seems, and nobody has the guts to ask his brother or whoever lives with him in that ramshackle old farmhouse.

All anyone really knows about him now is that he walks. They call him the Tennessee Walker. This is a play on words; there is a horse breed called Tennessee Walker that's known for its fancy footwork and gait.

When I lived out there, I would go for runs or walks in a three-mile loop that took me past his house. When I came to his strip of road, the Tennessee Walker would always step aside, respectfully, and nod once as I passed him.

I also used to drive through that area on the way to and from work. On a whim once, I slowed down when I came to his house. He was there, and he stepped politely aside as usual. I stopped, rolled down my window, and called out to him.

"Excuse me!" I said. He ambled over, looking vaguely surprised.

"I was just wondering," I said, "why do you always walk back and forth across the road?"

"Exercise," he said, after a pause.

"But why don't you go up and down or around the block instead of across?"

"Well…" He thought for a moment, as if the idea had never entered his head. "I don't rightly know."

And that was the only answer I ever got. "Okay," I said, and drove away.

Trying to understand what envy is like makes me think of the Tennessee Walker. An envious person is never still either. Laziness isn't the problem. Apathy isn't the problem. If anything, she is hyperactive—always moving, always striving, always alert, always watching those around her.

But her energy is being spent into an empty and bottomless pit. She is full of zeal, but not zeal for worshipping God and enjoying him. It is zeal for equality and for her own glory. She is an inexhaustible sentinel, watching for unfair blessing on other people. Again and again and again she will walk herself through the same vengeful fantasies, the same attempts to disguise or insult another person's advantage.

Envy is a repetitive, futile, obsessive walk across and across the same strip of road. You think you are doing the same thing as all the other runners and walkers you see, but you aren't. The motion is the same, but you will look up 20 years from now and realize that you are still on the same ten-foot strip of blacktop. One day you will find that in all your pursuits and surface conversations and private thoughts, you've been monotonously speaking the same refrain over and over and over: *If anyone has it, I ought to have it.*

"Why do you do that?" someone might ask you. "Why do you walk all day long? You're always moving, but you never turn yourself in an actual direction and get somewhere! You could have walked across the country by now. Why are you still walking in front of your house?"

"Well," you'd say, "because I can't stand the fact that my friend just ran a marathon."

Discussion Questions

- Do you remember any childhood lessons that you had in fairness? If so, what were they? Is fairness something you still find yourself concerned about?

- What are some of the ways you see people try to level out inequalities in the world today?

- How do you understand the distinction between envy, jealousy, and covetousness?

- What have been your experiences with envy so far in your life?

- Does it surprise you to recognize that you struggle with the sin of envy, especially knowing what a destructive and ungenerous impulse it is? Or conversely, is it so foreign to you that you have trouble relating?

3

Borrowed Dust:
The Envy of the Body

*While bodily training is of some value, godliness
is of value in every way, as it holds promise for the
present life and also for the life to come.*

1 TIMOTHY 4:8

The most beautiful girl I ever saw in real life was Evelina Nieminen. She was a foreign exchange student from Finland who showed up in my youth group one day when I was about 13.

She was willowy and small, shaped like an adult fairy. Her warm blonde hair looked delicate enough to have been made of feathers, always parted serenely on the side. Her face was shaped like an almond, with eyes that were unnaturally large set under a high forehead. She had eyebrows to sink a thousand ships. Her lips had sort of a Michelle Pfeiffer thing going on—it wasn't largeness that made them so striking; it was the totally unique shape of them.

She looked like she belonged in a snowdrift wearing a hooded mink coat or maybe in a field of flowers. When you looked at her, you thought of forests and of stage lights, of the house next door and of far-off lands. She had an accent and a small, throaty, purring tone of voice. She said cute, endearing things. And she spoke quietly, so everybody had to stop talking in order to hear her. People stopped talking around her a lot.

How we all wanted to be Evelina! And she knew it. From the first time she walked through the church doors, she seemed to accept with a sort of pleased surprise that all of us were starstruck.

I still remember the modest glances she would give the boys she allowed to take her on dates. They were always cut to the side, as if she wanted to protect them from the full effect of turning her face on them. And I remember the way those boys would act once they had been granted the honor of accompanying her somewhere. They were startled with their luck, and when they entered a room with Evelina, there was always this one second when the guy would make eye contact with his buddies and then look away. They weren't bragging; they were just making sure it was seen. *Yes, I'm on a date with this girl.*

I wondered at some point whether everyone in Finland was beautiful or if she was exceptional there as well. Her quiet acceptance of being made much of told me she was probably a favorite at home too.

I didn't hate her or really want to take her place, except in a very indistinct, daydreamy way. She was too far out of my sphere for that. It would have been like hating HRH Kate Middleton. But if she had been closer to me—a girl my age or a classmate—I think I would have struggled mightily to be civil.

After all, I felt awkward and a little chubby at that age, as most girls will tell you. I'd just sprouted tall, but was still carrying a left-over impression that I was built like a truck—strong and solid, with good square hands and a round face. My hair was naturally curly (naturally big), and my hips had long been called "childbearing hips" by my mother. (A note on childbearing hips: When you are 13, you can't help but feel that childbearing hips are a liability. It's nothing against children, or even the bearing of children, but when you have no immediate plans to bear them, the requisite hips can seem like overkill.)

I should also note that dressing oneself is a huge conundrum for someone who has the tastes of a tween and the body of a 30-year-old mother of three. Plus, I was homeschooled, while all the other girls in that youth group were private school girls with athletic limbs and pert ponytails. They seemed to get along very easily with one another.

Here is the really curious thing that began to happen.

I truly began to believe—beyond the shadow of doubt—that if I were thinner I would be one of them. For some reason, things had gotten mixed up in my mind that way, and the more socially frustrated I became, the more mixed up I got.

With utter clarity of purpose, I lived with the conviction that being thin equaled being pretty, and being pretty equaled being social. This was the only thing that divided me from them. It was a formula. It had never occurred to me that friendships and social comfort are complex and multifaceted or that people are generally more interested in how you feel about them than in whether your shirt lies flat over your lower-tummy bump.

Now, if this particular blindness had not burrowed into my heart, together with all the idolatry that was bound up in it, things might have run their course after middle school. This particular way of comparing yourself with others is especially strong, after all, in young people. Maybe it's because teens are still sort of new in their bodies—the limbs are still deciding how long to be, the face is still trying to get a balance between dry and oily, the curves are just getting settled.

But depending on your circle and the idolatries of your heart, this madness may continue into adulthood.

I've often found it true that the idolatries of a person's heart don't become apparent until the person stops getting what they want. When I began to feel the beauty pulling away from my grasp, my response was telling. The outward, visible action that I resorted to showed the inward, invisible idolatries that I already worshipped.

I was a habitual overeater even as a child, but as an emotional teen it got worse. I gained weight. I dieted. If you have ever dieted, you know that nothing encourages overeating like dieting does. Dieting as a young girl may be the worst way there is to *not* become an overeater. Soon, I was bargaining with myself over food. I had already formed ideas that there were "good" foods and "bad" foods. There were experiments, I remember—just little games—with how little I could eat.

You must know where this is going. This is a story I've read myself now, dozens of times, on blogs and in self-help books and in magazines. *Bulimia* was a word I learned through one of those magazines. I also learned how to do it, ironically, through one of those magazines—in a feature story on how to help the bulimic.

It was my sophomore year of college. When I finally tried this, it was after months and months of depressed, out-of-control bingeing. My family life had taken some hits, and my spiritual life was a wash. I was one "tossed to and fro…and carried about by every wind of doctrine" (Ephesians 4:14). I was "double-minded" and "unstable in all [my] ways," in fact (James 1:8). I worshipped food with my body even as I worshipped the body with my mind. My desires were at odds—food or thinness? Social interaction or lonely hiding? I wanted it all. This is a recipe for what the world calls low self-esteem and what the Bible calls walking in "the desires of the flesh" (Galatians 5:16-17).

I still remember the misery of catching glimpses of myself in a mirror, the lengths I would go to avoid having my picture taken. I could not stand the evidence before me. My face, my waist, my arms, my legs—every part of me had taken on soft, moving, undefined lumps of human flesh. I detested it.

One day after an afternoon of "food-hopping"—going from one free food event to another so that no one group of people would know how full I already was—I sought physical and mental relief from the fullness. I walked into the dorm bathroom, looked around miserably to see that no one was nearby, and grabbed my toothbrush.

It was very unpleasant. I didn't try it again for nearly a year.

Three years later, I was doing it every day. If I had to estimate, I'd say that I vomited between 500 and 800 times between the ages of 19 and 23.

This struggle was rooted in covetousness from the beginning. I wanted to be beautiful—so that I could be the most beautiful in rooms that I entered. I wanted to be thin—because I'd seen it on other people. But at this stage, the envy was still a general feeling without specific or prolonged targets. If I felt too uncomfortably bitter about the body of any one girl, I could easily distance myself from her. I compared myself to people in passing. If asked, I would have called it insecurity, not envy.

One day, though, the envy took a very personal turn.

The Birth of Dust Envy

I remember vividly a moment when I experienced intense envy of someone's physical body. I call this "dust envy," because our physical bodies are created from dust, the Bible tells us, and to dust our bodies will return (Genesis 2:7; 3:19).

I moved into a room with three of my sisters—sisters I had been nearly out of touch with during the years I'd been away at college. It's a strange thing to turn around and notice that someone has come up from behind and changed on you. If I hadn't been such an idolatrous, envious person, I would have been able to look at my younger siblings who had matured and rejoice. I would have given them a high five and gotten to know them.

But I was, so I didn't.

One day I was sitting on the bed reading, and one of my sisters came into the room. She picked out clothing without a moment's thought, threw it on, and walked out. Suddenly, I found that my hands were clutching the quilt on the bed in fury. My heart felt like it was breaking.

She was just perfect, that was all. It all hit me in a moment. Everything I had wanted even when I was younger and still pretty thin and people were telling me casually (the way women do) that I should model or something. Even then, I'd known that there was something a little off about my shape—too much like one of those Greek statues, not shaped the way people are supposed to be shaped in today's world.

It was time that I mourned and boiled over while I sat there. Time and toil, wasted. I had chased it for almost ten years, while she had never thought about it twice…and it was hers anyway. She had the body I wanted.

I've said several embarrassing things already, but this is the one I'm most ashamed of: After that day, I began wishing I could wreck her somehow. I wanted her to suffer, just a little. I wanted her to have a few moments or weeks or even months of not being so certain. I wanted to make her uncomfortable about something.

Now, it's part of the science of envy that the person's personality does play into the whole thing. A person who is too sweet, too kind to you, or too uncertain of themselves is much harder to envy. But a person who refuses to let a single crack show is—for me—hard not to want to take down.

It showed up in subtle ways. It showed up more in silence than anything else. When others praised, I was conspicuously silent. She didn't praise me either, I reasoned—why should I put myself out? Over time, it was hard to control the urge to subtly condemn, to find fault. As the saying goes, "To find out a girl's faults, praise her to her girlfriends."

Unfortunately, the envy never stayed quite as secret as I wanted it to. As the years passed, I began to sense enmity between us. I became sure I wasn't the only one who knew about it, but still my envy made me feel that I was the vulnerable one. How could I make an overture of friendship? I was the one with the felt disadvantage. *She must know that,* I thought.

It was years later that our feelings softened toward each other to the point that we could sit down and have an honest conversation about what had happened to our relationship. A white flag was run up, and we tentatively, slowly, came out from behind the barricades.

What was happening in my heart during all that time? Something that Paul warned the Galatians against carefully:

> Walk by the Spirit, and you will not gratify the desires of the flesh. For the desires of the flesh are against the Spirit, and the desires of the Spirit are against the flesh, for these are opposed to each other, to keep you from doing the things you want to do. But if you are led by the Spirit, you are not under the law. Now the works of the flesh are evident: sexual immorality, impurity, sensuality, idolatry, sorcery, enmity, strife, jealousy, fits of anger, rivalries, dissensions, divisions, envy, drunkenness, orgies, and things like these. I warn you, as I warned you before, that those who do such things will not inherit the kingdom of God. But the fruit of the Spirit is love, joy, peace, patience, kindness, goodness, faithfulness, gentleness, self-control; against such things there is no law. And those who belong to Christ Jesus have crucified the flesh with its passions and desires.

If we live by the Spirit, let us also keep in step with the Spirit. Let us not become conceited, provoking one another, envying one another (Galatians 5:16-26).

Let me call things the way Scripture calls them. I was sowing to the flesh instead of the spirit. This means that in everything I was pursuing the works of the flesh, which according to Paul, can be recognized a mile away: Sensuality. Idolatry. Enmity. Jealousy. Fits of anger. Rivalries. Envy. Then he specifically warns against envy again at the end of this passage, connecting it with conceit.

I was hating my sister. There is not another honest thing to call it. If you wish ill on another person and do not, at an essential level, root for them, you are hating them. And all of this was over a body so temporary that, unless the Lord returns, will likely be underground in the next 70 years. It will be unrecognizable to me in 30.

Four Things We Know About the Body from Scripture

To help us deal with our tendency to envy other people's physical appearance or ability, let's take a look at what the Bible teaches us about our bodies.

1. God Created Our Bodies on Purpose to Image Himself

Perhaps God could have made us pure spirits like himself. Apparently he doesn't object to the idea, since he created millions of them (they're called angels). But with us, God did something new. He created a double combo of soul *and* body. Something that could contemplate the cosmos *and* cast a shadow. A being that could ponder the ocean depths *and* displace water.

In this way, we image the God who is spirit only, as well as imaging the God who became a human like us. Think about this—our eyes see, and in this way, we image God, who sees. Our ears hear, and in this way, we image the God who hears. But our basic anatomy is also eternally significant: it was the shape God chose, knowing Jesus would wear it one day.

I have heard Christians say things like, "You're not a body who has a soul. Rather, you're a soul who lives in a body." There is just enough truth in this statement to make it plausible. It's true that when our bodies die, our spirits continue to exist in either heaven or hell. And for Christians, it's true that "though our outer self is wasting away, our inner self is being renewed day by day" (2 Corinthians 4:16). This is why we should never sacrifice our souls in order to save our bodies (Matthew 10:28). All Christians must be prepared for the day that we could be required to give up comforts, health, or even our lives for the sake of the gospel.

But what the creation account does teach is that, from the beginning, *the human body and soul were meant to go together*. Adam was not meant to be another angel. Without his soul, his body was dead. But without his body, God would have had nothing to breathe the breath of life into.

God meant for us to be embodied creatures. We are not failed angels, nor is the body a prison for the soul (though in a fallen world it will often feel like one). The body is good. Eyes and ears, hands and hair, breasts and bones, lungs and livers, tongues and toes. They are all good. Being visible, tangible, audible, and smellable is good. It is a privilege to be able to use one's body for the glory of God: to comb one's hair, to stir a risotto, to swing a bat, to run a 5K, to dance a waltz, to clothe oneself. It's good to be embodied—to be human.

When dealing with body envy—worshipping your neighbor's body and feeling ingratitude for your own—it can be tempting to respond by demeaning the body as though it were incidental to being human. But this is a false move. You can't cure envy by replacing it with scorn. And it's no good trading a materialist idolatry of the body for a gnostic idolatry of the soul.

It's glorious to have a body. Glorious and natural. God meant for it to be that way.

2. Beauty and Physical Strength Are Real and Unevenly Distributed

I'm not interested in pretending that beauty and physical strength are illusions. "Beauty is in the eye of the beholder" is true in a sense but also absolutely not true in another sense. Everybody knows that some people are better looking than others, and everybody knows that some people are better athletes.

Even the Bible speaks very matter-of-factly about physical attributes like these. Sarah was "beautiful in appearance" (Genesis 12:11), Vashti was "lovely to look at" (Esther 1:11), Rebekah was "attractive in appearance" (Genesis 26:7), Esther "had a beautiful figure and was lovely to look at" (Esther 2:7), and Rachel was "beautiful in form and appearance," unlike her sister Leah, whose "eyes were weak" (Genesis 29:17).

Joseph "was handsome in form and appearance" (Genesis 39:6), David was "ruddy and had beautiful eyes and was handsome" (1 Samuel 16:12), and of Saul it was said, "There was not a man among the people of Israel more handsome than he" (1 Samuel 9:2). Saul was also taller than any of the other people around him, according to the text.

In contrast, our Lord himself, when he became a man, was described as having "no form or majesty that we should look at him, and no beauty that we should desire him" (Isaiah 53:2). To say that Jesus wasn't good looking is to admit two obvious things:

First, there are more and less attractive people, and this is not all subjective to time and place.

Second, the physical appearance of a person doesn't tell us anything about his merit or righteousness.

So to tell the envious person that everybody is beautiful in their own way is not very helpful, and in my opinion, only heals the wound of the envious person lightly (Jeremiah 6:14; 8:11). Because, well, the envious person will know that you are lying.

3. Beauty Is Vain and Fleeting

What we just said about Jesus in the above section brings us to a very obvious next point: The Bible weighs the value of outward beauty very differently from the way the world does.

The wisdom writer notes that "charm is deceitful, and beauty is vain" (Proverbs 31:30). It's much better, he said, to be "a woman who fears the LORD." This passage even seems to imply that there is something disadvantageous about charm and beauty—because charm deceives and beauty is easily abused and overrated.

The hidden person of the heart is to be valued more than outward appearance. Listen to what the apostle Peter said to Christian wives:

> Do not let your adorning be external—the braiding of hair and the putting on of gold jewelry, or the clothing you wear—but let your adorning be the hidden person of the heart with the imperishable beauty of a gentle and quiet spirit, which in God's sight is very precious (1 Peter 3:3-4).

Notice *why* this passage says inner beauty is so precious: Unlike outward beauty, inner beauty is *imperishable*. Outward beauty perishes as our bodies age and run down. But inner beauty has eternal significance. The apostle Paul reasoned in a similar way about bodily exercise and training:

Train yourself for godliness; for while bodily training is of some value, godliness is of value in every way, as it holds promise for the present life and also for the life to come (1 Timothy 4:7-8).

Notice that Paul didn't condemn all bodily training; he simply put it in its proper place—"of *some* value," when compared to training in godliness, which is "of value in *every* way."

Scripture does the same thing with its treatment of beauty. Rather than dismissing physical beauty or never mentioning it, Scripture assigns it its *proper* value. That's the difference between the Bible's view of outward beauty and the world's view: The world places an *improper* value on outward beauty. It ranks it higher than it should.

We do the same thing when we refuse to acknowledge the varied levels of physical attractiveness in people. If we can't smile and wholeheartedly agree when someone makes a throwaway comment about their friend's daughter being beautiful, it may be that we've already swallowed the world's view of beauty. Worshipping something with obsessive discussion and pursuit is one way to idolize it. Another way is to give it inordinate power by pretending hard that it doesn't exist.

4. There Will Be Variety in Heaven

It is tempting to imagine that in heaven—a place with no disappointments—everyone's body will be equally strong, equally agile, equally graceful, or equally curvy. After all, the terrible things that happened to our bodies when Adam fell will be done away with in the new heaven and new earth, right?

But this is only partially true.

It's only partially true because some of our bodily differences amount to good, healthy variety. It's a good thing to have blondes and brunettes, dark skin and light, and bodies that are tall and short, muscular and skinny, curvy and straight. We will see it as the good variety that it actually is when we are in our sinless state (and *People* magazine is thrown into the lake of fire). These bodily differences—an essential feature in the glorious cross-cultural, pan-historical society of heavenly worshippers—will exist even when Christ's kingdom comes.

But other bodily differences will be done away with, because all suffering will be done away with.

There's a world of difference between being unable to walk and being unable to make the track team, between having a withered hand and being all thumbs. It's one thing to be deaf and another to have big ears; one thing to have no legs and another to have two left feet; one thing to have breast cancer and another to be flat-chested.

Although the line between the two categories can be fuzzy, it is still real. To help you see the line more clearly, ask yourself questions such as, *Can I imagine Jesus walking around Galilee healing people who were unhappy with the size of their noses? How do I think Jesus would have responded to a man who asked Jesus to make him 6'5" instead of 5'5"? Would paradise mean the absence of all that I currently dislike about my body, or would it mean the absence of all my insecure, comparison-driven, discontented feelings toward my body?*

If the bodily inequality that you struggle over is disease, deformity, or handicap, then you can comfort yourself with a promise that these things will be done away with. All of creation groans now (Romans 8:22), waiting for its day of deliverance from evils like these.

But for the person struggling under inequalities of another kind—his best friend is a star basketball player and he is five-foot-nothing and hanging out on the bench—other kinds of truth need to be spoken.

The solution to height envy is not to wish that everyone was brought down or up to your size. Nor is it to look forward to the day when all height inequality will be thrown into the lake of fire. (Do we really want an army of identical men and women in the new heaven and new earth anyway?)

While it may seem appealing to think of your new body as the body of your dreams or the body you've always wanted, this presumes that your dreams are untainted by sin and that what you want is what is best. Whatever else may be true, you can be sure of this: If your new body turns out to be shorter or slower or less athletic than someone else's, then you won't mind in the least because you will finally be free of all traces of envy and filled with all the fullness of Christ (Ephesians 4:13).

You will then drink a draft of contentment that you have only sipped from here. You will finally be free of your self-absorption and free to enjoy the stunning glory of those around you.

Corruption will put on incorruption, the natural will put on the spiritual, and envy will be swallowed up in glory.

Discussion Questions

- Have you ever experienced dust envy, the envy of someone else's athleticism or beauty?

- Do you think that you are more tempted to underemphasize the body ("we're just spirits with flesh on") or overemphasize the body ("physical health is of most vital importance")?

- What kinds of white lies have you heard people tell to minimize physical differences between people?

- What is it that you think a better body would get you?

- What kind of body have you imagined you will have in heaven? In what ways, if any, has this chapter shaped your thoughts about your heavenly body?

4

Borrowed Magnets: The Envy of Charm and Influence

*He smiled understandingly—much more than understandingly.
It was one of those rare smiles with a quality of eternal
reassurance in it, that you may come across four or five times
in life. It faced—or seemed to face—the whole eternal world
for an instant, and then concentrated on you with an irresistible
prejudice in your favor. It understood you just as far as you
wanted to be understood, believed in you as you would like to
believe in yourself, and assured you that it had precisely the
impression of you that, at your best, you hoped to convey.*

F. SCOTT FITZGERALD, *The Great Gatsby*

D uring a stressful political season, a middle-aged governor—
we'll call him Governor Smith—hired a bright young intern
from a rural area. We'll call him David Johnson.

David immediately showed signs of being exceptional at politics. He was likeable, clearheaded, and unafraid. He was honest and handsome, and he stuck to his values. The governor liked him so well that he soon promoted him into the circle of his closest employees, consultants, and confidants. The young man stayed humble and worked hard.

It was election season. Although the governorship wasn't on the line, there were a number of state senate and state representative positions coming open, as well as hundreds of local government spots. The parties warred against each other. One senator who could have been easily reelected instead announced his intention to run for governor in another two years. He laid down the gauntlet and began dropping insults and challenges. It was part of his fervor for his party in the current election, but it was also part of his plan to get a running start on the governorship.

David bloomed under this attack on his employer. No one else knew what to do with the style of attack that was being used, but David took over the PR department and parried every attack with class, integrity, and humor. He called out the opponent again and again, and he also did a great deal of good for the state senators and representatives in his party who were running hard for their own positions.

In the end, the election was a landslide victory for the party, and David was at the heart of it all. Governor Smith knew that a lot of the victory was due to the young man's brilliance and hard work. He gave him a nice watch and thanked him publicly in a meeting with his staff. David bowed his head and said simply, "Thank you. It's been a privilege." No bluster, no bragging—just an easy recognition that he had done well and that he was honored to serve the administration.

One day soon after, the governor read an op-ed piece about his employee. The columnist called for David to run for governor in two years. "We couldn't do better," he said. Soon, influential people were tweeting about this idea: "Governor Smith=yesterday's politics. David Johnson=tomorrow's politics." There was also a meme with a picture of David giving a speech at a pep rally and the words, "Governor Smith has the future governor of this state working for him."

The following month, Governor Smith overheard some women talking at the office. They were full of crushing praise for the young man. This bothered him, oddly. Smith was still an attractive man himself—he remembered his early rise in politics and the way women had talked about him then. And he was still almost a head taller than any man in any room he entered. It shouldn't have bothered him. But it did.

A kind of curling frustration was born in his belly. It grew into rage.

One night at dinner, his son asked where David was. It had been the governor's habit to invite David to family dinner at least once a week, but he'd given up making the invitation for almost a month. His teenage daughter dropped her fork, and he realized she was looking up expectantly too. With both sets of eyes on him, Governor Smith threw down his napkin and stormed away from the table.

His resentment began to grow out of control. David was too liked, too influential, too successful at everything he tried, too attractive to everyone he met. There was an indelible charm in the young employee, made up of untouchable "golden boy" factors that caused everybody who knew him to say, "That guy is going places."

In short, David's influence was dangerous. The hatred built up in Governor Smith until he couldn't see straight. He gave in to it completely. Finally, as the newspapers later reported, Smith hired somebody to kill the young man.

David, who would never have entered the race against the governor, managed to elude multiple attempts on his life, all paid for by his former employer. Instead of being killed, he ended up with the sympathy and loyalty of the whole state and successfully ran for governor later on. But even this was only after a thwarted Governor Smith committed suicide. David had always refused to run against him.

Influence and Charm

You probably recognized that as a true story, with some identifying details changed. It actually happened in Israel, in about 1020 BC.

Governor Smith was a king by the name of Saul, and David John-son just went by David. Later he came to be known as King David.

It's a slippery concept that we're trying to address in this chapter, but you'll know it when you see it. Some people have a kind of magnetic pull in their chests, some kind of *it* factor that holds sway over those around them. They have a charm that you may have trouble putting your finger on. All you know is that where they go, other people follow. Even you are inexplicably drawn to them.

I'm going to do a basic sketch, purely out of my own observation, of some of the different kinds of charm I have encountered through the years.

The Magnetic Pull of Humor

Humor draws people. You don't have to be a stand-up comedian to find an audience—wherever you find people, you find people who are willing and waiting to laugh. If you are a funny person, you will find people who are drawn to you solely for that reason. Like the other charms, this is a mixed blessing.

The men in my family have a gift for dry humor and storytelling. My brothers, father, uncles, and cousins sit around and sharpen wits on each other for fun by the hour. All the rest of us have to do is sit in the same room. No gathering would be the same without this element.

The Magnetic Pull of Frankness

Frank people possess an open and honest temperament. They are more likely to say what everyone else is thinking. They are more likely to confess foibles and sins of their own, but in such an easy way that you start feeling like your foibles maybe aren't so bad.

Some of them delight in open conversation and have a knack for asking questions that ease the honesty right out of you too. One of my husband's best friends is this way. He has a passion for asking people to share personal information with him. Everyone who goes through this gauntlet with him comes out feeling that there is something refreshing and unusual about it.

The Magnetic Pull of the Piercing Gaze

Some people can spend a few moments of quiet conversation with you and—with a steady gaze—make you feel as if they have ultimately seen and understood you. This quality is mentioned in the epigraph that opens this chapter, from *The Great Gatsby*: Gatsby is described as having a smile that "understood you just as far as you wanted to be understood, believed in you as you would like to believe in yourself, and assured you that it had precisely the impression of you that, at your best, you hoped to convey."

The flip side of this quality, in my experience, is very easy to envy and resent. If a person has a quiet gaze that seems to see and understand everyone, and that person then withholds approval from you—for some possibly legitimate reason—he soon becomes unbearably offensive to you. You don't care what he thinks anyway, you tell yourself. Why does he get to sit on this high horse of judgment on you? This effect is usually more egregious if the person also possesses a virtue that you don't possess, such as competence or self-control.

The Magnetic Pull of Happiness

I went to college with a guy whose charm completely consisted of his happiness. He was like a totally contented dog. He was a large, loping fellow, with an uncomplicated view of the world.

He liked everyone, and he was pleased with his life. He wasn't a worrier; he wasn't overly given to guilt or social drama. Because of this sheen of easy happiness over his life, he was surrounded by people at all times. This was good because he liked other people.

The Magnetic Pull of Confidence

People will follow anyone who shows them enough confidence. If you seem to be unafraid, it is a magnetic quality to the fallen, fearful human beings around you. Since the garden when we threw off our Great Leader, insecurity plagues us, and we are all willing to follow just about anything that pounds its chest.

A person who shows no fear is a person other people file in to follow around. It's just that simple. On a social level, it can mean something as simple as getting quiet to listen when the person talks at the dinner table. But the power of the confident person can expand to the point of cult leadership or political dominance.

It's Not Your Party

Paul Tripp tells a story about a kid's birthday party he attended. A little boy was there as a guest, but he tried to elbow in on the proceedings. When presents were being opened, he wasn't satisfied with the small bag of favors he'd been given. The enormous pile of presents for the birthday girl seemed more exciting. As she started opening them, he began to make not-so-subtle sounds of discontent. Finally, a mom pulled him aside.

Tripp overheard her telling the boy, "It's not your party."[1]

I strongly identify with the guest at that party. It is really difficult for me to stand by and watch while someone else shows herself to be the most likeable, most fun, or most influential person in my social group. I want all the influence to be mine. I want all the parties to be my party.

The fact of the matter is that sometimes it's just not your party. Sometimes you are not the star in the room. Can you handle that? The battle against envy is about growing the kind of heart that rejoices over somebody else's party hat.

Four Things We Know About Charm from Scripture

To help us overcome this kind of envy, here are some cues from Scripture about the indelible quality of charm.

1. If People Are Magnets, Then Christ Is Gravity

I'm not going to talk about Christ's attractions in the kind of terms I used above to describe different kinds of human charm. Sure, I think we could make a strong case that Christ possessed many, if not all, of these charms. I think the biblical stories show that he had some combination of humor, frankness, the piercing gaze, happiness, confidence, and more.

But rather than showing ways that Christ was just like us, except more so, I'm going to talk about the unique way that Christ embodied his heavenly Father as a magnet of men. His magnetism is such that you could analogize it more accurately to gravitational pull.

First, we can see that during Jesus's life on earth, people clumped around him—sometimes by the thousands. He was followed by crowds throughout his earthly ministry. They listened to his words, they begged for his healing touch, and often they came to challenge and debate him. Like many of the glories, Jesus's attraction was such that even those who hated him found themselves drawing near in challenge. One way or another, he couldn't be ignored. This happened organically as he went about his Father's business.

But he also called some of his disciples specifically, and each time they dropped what they were doing and followed him:

> While walking by the Sea of Galilee, he saw two brothers, Simon (who is called Peter) and Andrew his brother, casting a net into the sea, for they were fishermen. And he said to them, "Follow me, and I will make you fishers of men." Immediately they left their nets and followed

him. And going on from there he saw two other brothers, James the son of Zebedee and John his brother, in
the boat with Zebedee their father, mending their nets,
and he called them. Immediately they left the boat and
their father and followed him (Matthew 4:18-22).

This response doesn't seem normal to us. People don't usually
quit their jobs, walk off the jobsite, and physically follow a man who
has just called to them while passing by. It's rare for a person to command other people in this way at all, but it's much rarer for them to
come—as if the call were inescapable.

And we may think that this inescapable call ended when Christ
died and was raised and went to intercede for us with the Father,
but it seems that the call lives on. And Jesus predicted that it would:
"All that the Father gives me will come to me," he said (John 6:37).
And, "I, when I am lifted up from the earth, will draw all people to
myself" (John 12:32). We learn in Romans that the Father and Son
have set up an unstoppable chain of salvation, of which the "call" is
one unbreakable, inexorable link:

> Those whom he foreknew he also predestined to be con-
> formed to the image of his Son, in order that he might
> be the firstborn among many brothers. And those whom
> he predestined he also called, and those whom he called
> he also justified, and those whom he justified he also glo-
> rified (Romans 8:29-30).

The word used to denote God's glory in the Old Testament
contains an element of this irresistible pull. *Kabod* is the Hebrew
word I have in mind; it is translated as "glory," and its literal meaning has to do with weight or heaviness. That means the honor
and majesty it denotes has a certain gravitational connotation,
wouldn't you agree? Like the sun, the massive *kabod* of God the

Father and Christ the Son exerts drawing power on everything in its path.

Using the word *charm* to describe God would be ridiculous and irreverent. It's not a big enough word. But I think we've seen that when we use *charm* to describe a human being—one of God's image bearers—we are talking about that person's ability to draw people to himself. That person is a little rusty magnet corresponding to God's thunderous gravity.

2. Charm Can Be as Deceitful as Beauty

Having a little bit of power over people can be dangerous—for you and for them. When you are able to make people like you or to influence or control them in a certain way, sometimes you start to feel as if maybe, just maybe, God can be similarly influenced by your charms. Charm blinds other human beings to our faults, and we are happy to believe that if no one else sees our sin, then our sin must not be that big of a deal.

But Scripture warns us of the blinding properties of charm and beauty in the same breath: "Charm is deceitful, and beauty is vain," says Proverbs 31:30. And Isaiah warns that when judgment falls, God won't be blinded by the charm that worked so well on our fellow humans.

> Evil shall come upon you,
>   which you will not know how to charm away;
> disaster shall fall upon you,
>   for which you will not be able to atone;
> and ruin shall come upon you suddenly,
>   of which you know nothing (Isaiah 47:11).

3. Enjoy a Charming Person in a Godly Manner

The goal for us, as Christians, is to rejoice in all the glories that God has poured into others. This means that the goal is for us to also enjoy a fine personality—laugh, engage, converse, admire. We can see God's own glorious fingerprint in it.

But there's a warning to go along with this goal. The warning I'm thinking of is from Psalm 1:

> Blessed is the man
>   who walks not in the counsel of the wicked,
> nor stands in the way of sinners,
>   nor sits in the seat of scoffers;
> but his delight is in the law of the LORD,
>   and on his law he meditates day and night
>   (Psalm 1:1-2).

The charming person can easily slip over a line and become a scoffer. Charisma is easy to misuse. At some point, you will probably encounter charisma that wants to control and draw you into dangerous, sinful territory. Think of the peer pressure you experienced as a young person. Think of the sway that another human being has over you when you want him or her to like you.

This is good reason to fear God, not man (Matthew 10:28) and to choose your close friends carefully. Scoffing can be heady, charming stuff. Unfortunately, it leads to death.

4. Imitate Christ, Not the Charming Personality

For the last several months, whenever I give my toddler hot food, I blow on it in front of her. "Hot," I say. She occasionally looks up at me with a twinkle in her eye and spit-blows on the food herself. She's in on the joke.

Today I had the oven on, and she toddled over to the stove to watch me. She put her hand on the front door of the oven, which is not hot enough to burn unless you leave your hand on it for a while.

"That's hot," I said absentmindedly. I looked over a few seconds later to see her spit-blowing diligently on the oven.

We are born imitators. If we aren't imitating good examples, then we will be imitating bad ones. It's that simple. It's impossible to pull our adoring eyes off one thing without placing them firmly on something else.

We must be willing to steer our eyes off poor examples and onto better examples, filling our minds with the kind of "normal" that we want to see in our own lives. If we watch and emulate silly, likeable people, then we will be more silly and perhaps more likeable. If we watch and emulate godly, joyful people, then we will be more godly, more joyful, and perhaps more likeable too.

This is just what the psalmist was doing in the Psalms passage we read above. After a warning about getting into a comfortable huddle with sin, he gives us something else to fix our eyes on. The person who rejects sin is blessed, he said, because

> his delight is in the law of the LORD,
>   and on his law he meditates day and night.
> He is like a tree
>   planted by streams of water
> that yields its fruit in its season,
>   and its leaf does not wither.
> In all that he does, he prospers (Psalm 1:2-3).

Love and imitate Christ, loving his law and seeking his approval over man's. This is what Paul did. He asked rhetorically, "Am I now seeking the approval of man, or of God? Or am I trying to please man? If I were still trying to please man, I would not be a servant of Christ" (Galatians 1:10). Paul knew that his Lord had said already, "No one can serve two masters" (Matthew 6:24).

We can imitate Christ, and we can imitate others who are well imitating Christ (1 Corinthians 11:1). Otherwise, we are wasting our time pursuing a borrowed glory that means little. Devoting our mental lives to the envy and imitation of charming people—for the sake of charm alone—is not only a waste of time, but it is also counter-productive to our spiritual health.

Paul would tell us that although charm is nice, love is far and away more valuable. He would take us by the shoulder and say, "I will show you a still more excellent way" (1 Corinthians 12:31).

Discussion Questions

- Humor, frankness, the piercing gaze, happiness, and confidence—did you recognize any of these descriptions of different types of charm? Can you think of any other kinds of charm that were not listed?

- In what ways do you identify with the little boy in the story who wanted all parties to be his party?

- Have you met a person who was both charming and ungodly? What about charming and godly? Describe what this person was like and how you felt when you were with him or her.

5

5

Borrowed Ideas:
The Envy of the Intellect

Among the mature we do impart wisdom, although it is not a wisdom of this age or of the rulers of this age, who are doomed to pass away. But we impart a secret and hidden wisdom of God, which God decreed before the ages for our glory.

1 CORINTHIANS 2:6-7

He sat in the aisle seat of the airplane, lanky and young. He was just a punk kid. He was careless in his movements and full of the exuberance that people wear when they know the best is ahead of them and everything good is headed their way.

He spent the first hour after takeoff letting me know what exactly he was, using matter-of-fact boasts. This was odd to me because I was only 13, and he was several years older; it showed that he was an equal-opportunity braggart. We were headed on a mission trip, part of the same youth group, but we had never spoken before. I was surprised to find that he knew my name, and I was preoccupied throughout the conversation with concealing the fact that I'd never flown before.

"I'm a National Merit Scholar," he said as a conversational opener.

"Oh?" I said lightly, trying not to seem impressed. "I don't know what that is."

He was genuinely surprised and mildly amused. "It's a full schol-arship that goes to any university. But usually people use them to go to really good schools. Only a few of them in the whole United States."

"Cool," I said, trying to turn back to my book. I was perilously shy of boys, and this was too much. He was forcing his bragging on me, which made me feel both gratified and defensive.

"You just take a test," he said then with clear, bright eyes, like it was a secret he'd discovered. "I took the ACT too. You know what I got? A perfect 36." Maybe he wasn't bragging after all; maybe he was trying to inspire me to work hard in school or something.

"I like aerodynamics best," he said then, as if I had asked him. "Do you want to know how this plane is flying?" He proceeded to explain how the air was creating some kind of circular force on a certain part of the wing, whipping up and over it—the details are as fuzzy to me now as they were then. It seemed incredible to me—as I peered out of the tiny window and watched the wing juxtaposed over a ground that was toyishly small—that this magic trick he was describing held us in the air. The fact that he could explain it made me feel almost as if he were the one responsible for it.

I didn't understand. But I acted as if I did, and I acted as if it wasn't fascinating at the same time. I yawned and waited for him to get tired of bragging and go to sleep, which he did a little while later.

But after he went to sleep, slumped over on his tray table like a giant, I thought about the wing and the scholarship and the 36. What must it be like to understand the wing of a plane and to be going to college and to know that whatever you wanted to do you could probably do, because you had scored absolutely perfectly on the cleanest test of academic excellence that America has? What must it be like to be 18 and to have all that right there in your hands? I suppose you'd want to brag about it. And I realized then that if he wanted to brag I wouldn't get too mad at him, because maybe he'd worked really hard at the ACT and maybe he was really interested in the wing of the plane.

But as soon as he woke up, I found myself immediately on the defensive again. He struck up a conversation about music after that, and I was so busy trying not to let my ignorance show—I didn't know any of the names he was using so casually (Coltrane and John Denver and The Police)—that I slipped right back into monosyllables.

But beneath my rigid refusal to be impressed, I could feel my mind whirling. Could I get a scholarship? Could I find out about Coltrane and John Denver? Could I get a good ACT score? Would I be able to swagger and laughingly brag and fall asleep on a tray table unselfconsciously if I had the power of his mind?

Then I began to think about this guy's siblings. His classmates. If he was this open with me, a stranger, about his advantages—so cheerfully frank about his brain—then how did he talk about it to them? And how did they feel about it? Surely this boy's easy confidence felt like a kick in the teeth to at least a dozen people in his life. Perhaps he even knew it. Perhaps he liked it.

Do People Really Envy Intelligence Today?

As adults who have been out of school for some time, we can have difficulty remembering the years upon years we spent sitting in a classroom being intellectually measured against our peers. Many of us are no longer graded—not like that. Many of us no longer have to trudge through tasks that don't come naturally to us. We've found our groove, so to speak. We are working jobs that are fitted to our strengths, and no one is making us do long division. The prophecies that we whined to our parents when we were teens—"I'll never use this is in real life!"—have actually come true.

And this is as it should be. The academic world is usually a training ground, and not everyone is going to spend their lives reading for reading's sake or computing for computing's sake or debating for debating's sake.

But perhaps you've never quite left those hallways behind. You still have friends who live intellectual lives, either through work or in their spare time. You engage them. You listen to them talk, or if you're in a sharp minority, you look over their mathematical algorithms and note that the work has been done correctly. And as you do these things, you find that there is still a running GPA in your mind. They continue to get As, seemingly without effort. And you continue to work yourself half to death for a B.

Contrary to those cries of "I'll never use this in real life," you see that they are using those academic skills. Their intellect helps them in their work. It helps them in conversation. How smoothly they talk about things and how clearly they can walk circles around other people without even meaning to do so! It helps them financially—they may have the mental horsepower for the stock market, for entrepreneurship, for programming, or for communicating their way into money. Or perhaps their actual education continues to follow them—maybe they graduated from an institution that basically guarantees a future of gainful employment and social stature.

The glory of the human mind has been blown out of proportion by idolatrous mankind for thousands of years. We can feel the weight and pressure of intellect, and we know that it is something to contend with, something to be impressed by. But in the darkness of our understanding—as we have shut our eyes against the glory of the omniscient God—we have lost any sense of how limited and foolish the human mind really is.

The Christian world is no exception. It is also full of sinful people, and these people carry on their own secret struggles and rivalries within the subculture. If you have ever been a member of a church that values theological precision, you have probably experienced some of the pitfalls of intellectual pride. Many of the scriptures we are dealing with in these chapters make the most sense in the context of Christian community. There is a necessary struggle that comes with fighting to interpret and teach God's Word while also keeping a check on the pride of the human heart. Christians have "experts" too, and where there are experts, there are all kind of unnamed, secret rivalries.

Six Things We Know About the Mind from Scripture

God, who knows the human heart as he knows all things, provides guidance for those who would seek true wisdom.

1. Our Lord Used His Mind

Jesus was himself a learned man. He knew Scripture, and he knew it because he had studied. He had to study, because he was a man, and men start out as babies. Babies don't know Scripture. As Jesus became a man and got taller, he also prepared for ministry and teaching by growing in his knowledge of the written word (Luke 2:52).

Although we don't know how easy or hard all of this was for Jesus the man (with a brain that fired synapses just like ours), we do know that he had to put in effort and that the results were a glorious weight of wisdom and understanding. This is something that even unconverted readers of the Gospels recognize. After all, the thing Jesus is most often called by the secular world—in an insipid denial of his identity as the Son of God—is "a great teacher."

And it is something that even people in Jesus's hometown recognized, although they didn't particularly like it:

> He went away from there and came to his hometown,
> and his disciples followed him. And on the Sabbath he

began to teach in the synagogue, and many who heard him were astonished, saying, "Where did this man get these things? What is the wisdom given to him? How are such mighty works done by his hands? Is not this the carpenter, the son of Mary and brother of James and Joses and Judas and Simon? And are not his sisters here with us?" And they took offense at him. And Jesus said to them, "A prophet is not without honor, except in his hometown and among his relatives and in his own household" (Mark 6:1-4).

Jesus wasn't able to do many signs in the face of such unbelief. He actually marveled because of their unbelief (6:6). So he left town. There's nothing like the vicious, envious talk of your childhood neighbors and family friends. Glory of any kind stands no chance in the old 'hood.

And lest we forget, envy is what prompted the chief priests to deliver Jesus up to his death (Mark 15:10). In a real sense, glory envy is what killed our Savior. And although it wasn't named specifically, the bundle of glories Jesus possessed included the power of the mind. He was sharp, although his wisdom sounded like folly to those who were perishing (1 Corinthians 1:18).

I simply bring up the mental capacity that Jesus displayed in order to make the point that one can be righteous at the same time as being smart and still be envied for it.

2. We Are Commanded to Use Our Minds

Scripture is clear about the fact that we should be students. Students use the power of the mind for study, and for Christians, the subject of our most intent study must be the Word of God. Paul wrote to Timothy about this very thing, giving one all-important reason for learning the Bible:

> Continue in what you have learned and have firmly
> believed, knowing from whom you learned it and how
> from childhood you have been acquainted with the
> sacred writings, which are able to make you wise for
> salvation through faith in Christ Jesus. All Scripture is
> breathed out by God and profitable for teaching, for
> reproof, for correction, and for training in righteous-
> ness, that the man of God may be complete, equipped
> for every good work (2 Timothy 3:14-17).

Paul connected Timothy's intellect with his faith in Christ. He said that Timothy's whole mind should be engaged in the study of the Word. Why? Because the Word is breathed out by God himself. To know God, Timothy must know the Word that God has breathed out. This means study; this means kicking his intellect into full gear—to love God with his heart, soul, strength, and yes, his mind (Luke 10:27).

The Christians in Berea were commended in Acts for their study of the Word. Here, their mental effort was also linked inextricably to faith. They studied, and this is why they believed:

> These Jews [in Berea] were more noble than those in Thes-
> salonica; they received the word with all eagerness, exam-
> ining the Scriptures daily to see if these things were so.
> Many of them therefore believed, with not a few Greek
> women of high standing as well as men (Acts 17:11-12).

And David described the process of guarding his way through a love of Scripture in Psalm 119. It sounds remarkably like studying:

> I have stored up your word in my heart,
>   that I might not sin against you.
> Blessed are you, O Lord;
>   teach me your statutes!

With my lips I declare
    all the rules of your mouth.
In the way of your testimonies I delight
    as much as in all riches.
I will meditate on your precepts
    and fix my eyes on your ways.
I will delight in your statutes;
    I will not forget your word (Psalm 119:11-16).

3. We Are Commanded to Guard Against Certain Uses of Our Minds

Paul warned Timothy against a certain kind of knowledge in another letter. "Guard the deposit entrusted to you," he said. "Avoid the irreverent babble and contradictions of what is falsely called 'knowledge,' for by professing it some have swerved from the faith" (1 Timothy 6:20-21).

It's clear from this warning that certain kinds of knowledge are not knowledge at all. Within the same passage, Paul alluded to a kind of person who deals in false knowledge. He urged Timothy to combat them with true wisdom, teaching and urging the gospel via Scripture:

> Teach and urge these things. If anyone teaches a different doctrine and does not agree with the sound words of our Lord Jesus Christ and the teaching that accords with godliness, he is puffed up with conceit and understands nothing. He has an unhealthy craving for controversy and for quarrels about words, which produce envy, dissension, slander, evil suspicions, and constant friction among people who are depraved in mind and deprived of the truth, imagining that godliness is a means of gain (1 Timothy 6:2-5).

The power of the mind, like all other glories that God lends, can be used for wickedness as well as for good. Here, it was being used to stir up controversy and win friends and money. Sound familiar? I have an image popping up in my mind of a university professor competing with his colleagues to see who can take their nihilism to the outermost limit. Then another image comes up—a celebrity pastor in a televised church, using a remnant of Christian truth to sell pop psychology and make a name for himself.

Some kinds of intellectual activity have nothing to do with wisdom and bring forth "envy, dissension, slander, evil suspicions, and constant friction" instead of the fruits of the Spirit. This kind of worldly endeavor knows no fear of God and craves only power over man.

4. We Need to Lay Our Hands on Our Mouths

The glory of human intellect, while a true glory that mirrors the glory of the unfathomable mind of God, is comparatively unimpressive. Human beings are confused, irrational, and often in the dark about even basic facts about the world around us. All of our studies, our libraries of books, our internet's worth of searchable knowledge makes us feel powerful. We have an illusory feeling that no matter what question arises, there is an expert for that, somewhere. Or an app for that.

But in reality, our understanding of even the finite, measurable things of earth often amounts to the conjectures of a group of kindergarteners who theorize about what makes the rain. They have words to describe the rain—it's "wet" or it "drops from the clouds"— but they are really just making observations about the wonder that is rain.

Mankind can't even understand itself.

Think of the billions of dollars and hours of study going into the field of psychology each year. Like kindergartners, we've named all the syndromes. We conduct new studies every year trying to figure out what's causing poverty, depression, and addiction. But how much progress have we made in explaining the human heart? Who can know it? What data can explain a father who quits every job he gets and finally abandons his children? Or a healthy 60-year-old woman in the upper middle class who can't stop drinking? When you consider the unbelievably vague expressions used to explain how Prozac works, you wonder just how much humans have really got nailed down.

We each live in a world of wonders among other humans who are, like ourselves, full of blatant inconsistencies and shocking weaknesses. Christians who consider themselves wise and understanding should practice the virtue of shutting up, remembering what Scripture says about many words:

> Be not rash with your mouth, nor let your heart be hasty to utter a word before God, for God is in heaven and you are on earth. Therefore let your words be few…For when dreams increase and words grow many, there is vanity; but God is the one you must fear (Ecclesiastes 5:2,7).

In the book of Job, God is the One dressing men down for opening their mouths against him. For about 70 verses, he soliloquizes on all the reasons that a wise man should be just wise enough to shut up.

> Then the LORD answered Job out of the whirlwind and said:
>
> > "Who is this that darkens counsel by words
> > without knowledge?…
> > Where were you when I laid the foundation
> > of the earth?
> > Tell me if you have understanding.
> > Who determined its measurements—
> > surely you know!" (Job 38:1-2,4-5).

5. God's Mind Is Infinitely Superior

That passage in Job—chapters 38 and 39 in their entirety—is a pounding mass of evidence that God's knowledge and power are untouchable. The poetry asks ironically if Job and his friends have "comprehended the expanse of the earth" or if they can "discern the paths" to the "dwelling of light" or have "seen the storehouses of the hail," implying that these are all things God has seen, understood, and wrought. "You know," said God sarcastically, "for you were born then, and the number of your days is great!" (Job 38:18-21).

Job's response to this demonstration of God's unlimited grasp and reach over the earth and heavens is simply this: "Behold, I am of small account; what shall I answer you? I lay my hand on my mouth" (40:4).

Then consider these beautiful claims made in the Bible about God's omniscience—his complete mental grasp and power over everything, everywhere.

> He determines the number of the stars;
> he gives to all of them their names.
> Great is our Lord, and abundant in power;
> his understanding is beyond measure
> (Psalm 147:4-5).

> I am God, and there is none like me
> declaring the end from the beginning
> and from ancient times things not yet done
> (Isaiah 46:9-10).

> By this we shall know that we are of the truth and reassure our heart before him; for whenever our heart condemns us, God is greater than our heart, and he knows everything (1 John 3:19-20).

For as the heavens are higher than the earth,
    so are my ways higher than your ways
    and my thoughts than your thoughts (Isaiah 55:9).

6. True Wisdom Comes Only Through Submission to God's Word and Is Accompanied by Virtue

Christians who consider themselves wise and understanding should recall the urging of the epistles to test all knowledge with good works:

> Who is wise and understanding among you? By his good conduct let him show his works in the meekness of wisdom. But if you have bitter jealousy and selfish ambition in your hearts, do not boast and be false to the truth. This is not the wisdom that comes down from above, but is earthly, unspiritual, demonic. For where jealousy and selfish ambition exist, there will be disorder and every vile practice. But the wisdom from above is first pure, then peaceable, gentle, open to reason, full of mercy and good fruits, impartial and sincere (James 3:13-17).

Meekness and good works must accompany wisdom—or else the wisdom is moot and probably false. The phrase in verse 17 is very helpful to us in diagnosing what kind of intellectual activity we're engaging in: Is it pure? Is it peaceable, gentle, open to reason? Is it full of mercy? What kind of fruit does it produce? Is it impartial and sincere?

Also, notice how clearly James understood that intellectual pursuits—even the Christians' intellectual pursuits—are prone to rivalries and jealousies. It's the first earmark he asked us to look for. Do you think you're wise? Really? Well, then, what about the jealousy and ambition in your heart? It's a warning sign that your wisdom is not the kind that comes from above.

Also, remember that the way the world sees wisdom will often be at odds with the wisdom that comes from above. When Christ came, he overturned the powers of the age. Accept this: Whatever the state of your mind, you aren't going to win intellectual accolades with the world through your belief in Christ. It just isn't going to happen, no matter how intellectually engaged your faith is. We won't look wise to those who are perishing, because the word of the cross is folly to them, according to 1 Corinthians 1:18.

The wisdom we have chosen is of a different kind, meant to bring humility to mankind. It will stand the test of time.

> Where is the one who is wise? Where is the scribe? Where is the debater of this age? Has not God made foolish the wisdom of the world? For since, in the wisdom of God, the world did not know God through wisdom, it pleased God through the folly of what we preach to save those who believe. For Jews demand signs and Greeks seek wisdom, but we preach Christ crucified, a stumbling block to Jews and folly to Gentiles, but to those who are called, both Jews and Greeks, Christ the power of God and the wisdom of God. For the foolishness of God is wiser than men, and the weakness of God is stronger than men (1 Corinthians 1:20-25).

It sounds like foolishness. God became a man, in order to save beings he created himself. This is life, and it involves death. This is wisdom, best understood by the mind of a child. It's not the kind of thing the Jews, the Greeks, the hipsters, the professors of philosophy, the Internet trolls, the op-ed musers, the politicians, the screenwriters, the health-and-wealth gospel TV preachers, or the guy with the big glasses and cool haircut can understand. They won't be drawn to it because of the big words we might have come up with in our (good and necessary) studies. If they're drawn to this message at all, it will be because of the simple, upside-down truth: Even the foolishness of God is wiser than men. Even his weakness is stronger than our strength.

For one foolish man to envy another foolish man's foolishness and pygmy intellectual pursuit is…

Well, it's foolishness.

Discussion Questions

- When you were in school, did you ever envy the smarter kids? If so, describe someone whose intelligence you envied and why.

- To what degree does someone's intelligence still matter to you in your everyday life?

- When you seek to humble yourself intellectually by beholding God's wisdom, how do you think that will affect your perspective of other people's intelligence? Have others' intellectual abilities ever become less intimidating to you as you seek God's wisdom?

6

Borrowed Money:
The Envy of Options

"Elinor, for shame!" said Marianne; "money can only give happiness where there is nothing else to give it. Beyond a competence, it can afford no real satisfaction, as far as mere self is concerned."

"Perhaps," said Elinor, smiling, "we may come to the same point. Your competence and my wealth are very much alike, I dare say."

JANE AUSTEN, *Sense and Sensibility*

Seriously? I'm your age, I'm making 15 bucks an hour, and you're shopping for six-hour stretches buying things that you don't need."

Years after the fact, Amy still remembered the way she used to feel about her employer. She worked for a young mother as a nanny when they were both about 23. Neither had grown up rich. But this young mother, whom we'll call Emma, had married an older and wealthy man. She had two children right away, and Emma hired my friend Amy as a nanny.

It was a relationship of unseen tension.

"She didn't work because she didn't have to," Amy said, tapping her fingers on my kitchen table. "It was amazing—she was the age of someone right out of college, and she was completely and fully supported in any hobby she would ever want to do. She could shop all day long, and not only did she have the money to pay for stuff that she saw, but she had someone she trusted at home keeping her children, cleaning her house.

"She had the convenience that I wanted. The ability to go out and do whatever she wanted at a moment's notice for however long she wanted. If, after a day of shopping, she came home and wanted to go out to the nicest restaurant in town with her husband, they'd just go. If they were out and didn't really feel like coming back at the agreed time, they'd call and say, 'We'll double your rate for you to stay over,' because they could do that.

"And her clothes! People recognized her for always being perfectly put together. She got to the point where she had so much, she had to give things away to make room for the new things. I got a taste of it, too, because she gave me a lot of things. And this fed my feelings.

"She was very beautiful to begin with. But there were certain physical characteristics that were increased because of her money. For instance, she could afford to get her hair highlighted every time it needed it. She changed her hair color constantly. She wore the best makeup and spent an hour and a half putting it on every morning while I watched her children. She could afford a personal trainer, so she was in shape; and she bought organic food, so they were all healthy.

"I could see her character flaws clearly because of my resentment. She wanted kids but didn't want to take care of them, so she could leave all day and experience a single life even though she was the mother of two. She could pay people to like her. She didn't have any good friends, but if she said, 'I'm having an awesome expensive Christmas party, and we're giving away gifts and having a nice caterer,' people would show up for that. People benefited from that close proximity to wealth.

"And the spending—sometimes I would just get angry about it. It wasn't specifically that I would have made a better decision in some big financial move; it was just, 'You're not looking at the big picture here.' I felt like she just had a shorter-term mind-set.

"She didn't have any good friends, so she treated me as a confidante rather than hired help. That was strange too. She was extremely self-conscious, always spending money on things that would help her fit in. And honestly, she wasn't very smart, so she connected only with people who were as shallow or as concerned with external things as she was, and people like that don't get along well."

When Amy had run out of things to say, she stopped abruptly and sat quietly, thinking. She hadn't hesitated for a moment in her description, as if it had just been waiting on her tongue. The taste seemed to still be in her mouth—that bewildering, bitter flavor of envy. She moved in her seat as if she could still feel the burning heat of living too close to another person's gloried lifestyle.

Amy said that she hasn't spoken to her former employer and "friend" in four years.

Money Is About Options

People are always surprised when they find out that they are materialistic. No one thinks they are. Americans love to talk about how materialistic Americans are, but it doesn't often hit home: *I am a lover of things. I am a lover of stuff.*

It's not really the green paper that you want, is it? It's what the paper can get you.

Money can be about all kinds of things. It can be about food; it can be about clothes or cars or houses; it can be about travel. It can be about power. It can be about education or having the option to do what you love, or about the convenience of not having to scrimp and budget.

Money, for most Westerners, is not about survival—it's about options. Even if we are talking about the option of not relying on the government dole, of buying real groceries instead of ramen. It's about leisure and convenience instead of worry and stress. Living tired and overworked or living rested and relaxed.

My envy in this arena of life has been less intense than in some of the others. More in passing, I guess. But it's still there, and it can also greatly exacerbate other envies that are already present. Already upset that my friend seems to know she is smarter than me, I may take it as a slap in the face when I see her upscale apartment for the first time. Or after years of low-grade envy over my cousin's artistic talent, I may feel an extra burst of discomfort when I hear that she just bought a ticket to Rome.

If this world is all we have, then envying another person's lifestyle isn't just understandable. It's logical.

A Word on Social Media

Today, we have the immense privilege of using the internet to find out about more things we don't have. People's ideas about luxury used to be limited to what they saw in their own communities. You could hate the guy with the nicest house in town, and you could compare your kids to the kids in your local church, but you weren't competing with the lifestyle of everyone in the world at once. But now we have a new opportunity—we can now envy people who don't even exist: The people our friends project onto the internet.

I've read several articles recently about "image-crafting," in which people have a version of themselves prepared for real life and another even more careful version for the internet. On social media, we can control exactly what people see of us. Pictures can be untagged, leaving only the ones of your good side. You can post artful statuses about your vacation ("Praise God for the beautiful Brazilian beaches he made!"), your promotion ("I'm officially assistant producer! #blessed"), or your happy marriage ("He brought me breakfast in bed today. #marriageisbliss").

Now, the life that another person has is one thing—and it may be an enviable thing in its own right. But you may never get that far. The beautiful, varied, monied existence he or she projects online is enough to turn your stomach.

She goes to parties with cool people—you've seen the friendship brags. She wears great clothing all the time—you've seen the pictures. She has a fantastic job that she enjoys every day of her life—you've seen the updates. She is never bored and never boring—you've seen the tweets. She is comfortable and rich, and you have the proof of it constantly hitting your newsfeed. It no longer takes actual money to appear wealthy. All you need is a smartphone.

The Village Mentality and the Fear of Success

Helmut Schoeck discussed the culture of envy in developing countries at some length in his 1969 book *Envy*.[1] He cited several separate studies on the social habits of villagers on the continents of South America, Africa, and Asia. In each of these distinct cultures, there was a common attitude of what he calls "institutionalized envy."

Schoeck told stories of women in Mexico who would avoid telling even family members about a new baby, a new dress, or a new article of furniture because they feared inciting envy. He told of men in Guatemala who would intentionally buy several small fields instead of one large field in an attempt to disguise good fortune. He described the assumption in Aritama, a Colombian Mestizo village, where inhabitants didn't believe in the possibility of natural death. If you die, they believed, it was because one of your neighbors was envious of you and hexed you with black magic.

In fact, many of the cultures Schoeck studied shared a strong belief in black magic. Because of this, the people would assume any bad thing that happens to a family—a failed crop, illness, or even a negative change in character—was a direct result of an envious neighbor's magic. Furthermore, a neighbor's success was also attributed to magic.

Under these conditions, men feared invoking the envy of their neighbors to the point of neurosis, but they also watched their neighbors with a constant, envious eye. Distrust reigned.

One sad result of this climate of institutionalized envy was that it hampered the growth of whole villages. No one could learn new trades when they risked the envy of their neighbors. Men feared to build a permanent brick house and fill a storehouse with savings because they risked the "evil eye." People didn't share tips on where to get a good trade deal, how to cook a dish more effectively, or how to cultivate a crop for a bigger yield. This would be drawing attention to your own success in buying, cooking, or farming. Children in one village in Mexico were even discouraged from sharing their things with others, because this was viewed as boastful. Many of the villagers believed that if you tried to help somebody, you were trying to get something in return.

This was more than 50 years ago, in places where poverty was the norm. Obviously, it feels foreign to the culture of excess that today's Western Christians are familiar with. But we can see from these descriptions that people everywhere are just people, given to the same kinds of sins, with the same sidelong glances and tendencies to dissatisfaction.

In the villages studied by these anthropologists, a prevailing sentiment was clear: *Every man for himself. Keep your cards close to your chest. Keep your head down. If you look like you've got something good going for you, someone is going to try to take it. And if somebody else starts to look a little too comfortable, you'd better keep a tight rein on them because their gain is your loss.*

Sound familiar?

Whether we're talking about a circle of moms in yoga pants, sliding subtle brags into conversation about where their family is vacationing this winter, or a circle of women hanging laundry in a Guatemalan village and gossiping about whose goat just had twins, the spirit of material comparison is as old as the exile from Eden.

Five Things We Know About Money from Scripture

As followers of Christ, we know that God has a great deal to say about the envy of material options.

1. God Owns Everything

God is omni-wealthy. This is perhaps the most basic of all biblical teachings about money and possessions. As David famously observed, "The earth is the LORD's, and everything in it, the world, and all who live in it" (Psalm 24:1 NIV).

How did God come by such massive wealth? Answer: He made it. Creation entails ownership. So the psalmist reasons:

> In his hand are the depths of the earth;
> 　the heights of the mountains are his also.
> The sea is his, for he made it,
> 　and his hands formed the dry land (Psalm 95:4-5).

God doesn't need our money. In the words of the apostle Paul, He "does not live in temples made by man, nor is he served with human hands, as though he needed anything" (Acts 17:24-25).

Truth is, God isn't nearly as impressed with your neighbor's wealth as you are.

2. God Disposes of His Wealth as He Sees Fit

God is sovereign over wealth and poverty. Not only does he own all things, but he also distributes them as he pleases. He controls all the world's resources and decision makers, and nothing happens on his watch that doesn't pass through his hand. In the words of Hannah, "The LORD makes poor and makes rich; he brings low and he exalts" (1 Samuel 2:7).

Let this sink in.

The Lord makes poor, and the Lord makes rich. Therefore, when you envy your prosperous neighbor, you are, at one level, begrudging God's generosity. When you feel resentful at your own financial lot, you are failing to trust the sovereign God. At such times, God's question for you is the same as that of the vineyard master in the parable: "Don't I have the right to do what I want with my own money? Or are you envious because I am generous?" (Matthew 20:15 NIV). Money envy, like all envy, must be confronted with the goodness and sovereignty of God.

But now for some necessary biblical nuances. Let's be clear about what God's sovereignty over wealth and poverty does not mean.

First, God's sovereignty does not mean that if you are rich, then God approves of you, and if you are poor, then God disapproves of you. God was also sovereign over Pilate, the Jewish leaders, and the Romans when they crucified Jesus (Acts 2:23; 4:27-28), but that doesn't mean that he approved of their actions. They were still "lawless men" (Acts 2:23). Remember Job's comforters, who mistakenly thought that people always get what they deserve and deserve what they get in this life (Job 4:7-8; 40:7).

On the contrary, Scripture is crystal clear that financial status is no sure indicator of spiritual status. The fact that it rains on our crops doesn't mean that God is pleased with you, because God "sends rain on the righteous *and the unrighteous*" (Matthew 5:45 NIV). The wicked man in Jesus's parable was "clothed in purple and fine linen and…feasted sumptuously every day" (Luke 16:19), but he still went to hell when he died. Lazarus went straight to paradise after a lifetime of brutal poverty (Luke 16:22).

Second, God's sovereignty does not mean that the poor should not seek to improve their lot. Fatalism is unbiblical, because the Bible always presents God's sovereignty as being compatible with human responsibility. God desires all of us to work hard to provide for our own needs and the needs of our families, so that we can "walk properly before outsiders and be dependent on no one" (1 Thessalonians 4:12).

Poor people must, of course, be careful not to look to money as their savior. But it is not wrong to seek to escape poverty, especially if your goal is to be able to have more to share (Ephesians 4:28). But the counsel of the psalmist always applies: "If riches increase, set not your heart on them" (Psalm 62:10).

God's sovereignty does not mean that our character, habits, and decisions have no bearing on our financial status. As a general rule, all else being equal, hard work does lead to prosperity and laziness does lead to poverty. You find this teaching especially in the book of Proverbs.

3. Wealth Can Be Hazardous to Your Soul

Whenever you envy a rich person, you are envying someone who will find serious challenges in escaping hell, because he is surrounded by threats to his soul. You're envying someone who is much more likely to be surrounded by yes-men (including pastors) who treat him with kid gloves, offer him the best seats (James 2:1), and stroke his ego, instead of faithfully reproving him for his sin.

There's another familiar passage, with a similarly strong warning, in Paul's letter to his protégé, Timothy.

> Those who desire to be rich fall into temptation, into a snare, into many senseless and harmful desires that plunge people into ruin and destruction. For the love of money is a root of all kinds of evils. It is through

this craving that some have wandered away from the faith and pierced themselves with many pangs (1 Timothy 6:9-10).

Now contrary to popular misquotings, Paul did not say that *money* is the root of all evil but that the *love of money* is a root of all kinds of evil. Money is not intrinsically evil, even in large doses. As we'll see later, wealthy people have an enriching role to play in God's church and God's world. But while money is both helpful and necessary, money love is fatal. Money love is like a gateway drug, leading to all kinds of evils: robbing banks, starting wars, mugging subway passengers, giving perjured testimony, committing adultery, showing favoritism, hacking email accounts, filming pornography, cheating on your taxes, selling your body, coveting your neighbor's stuff, and envying others' success.

The world doesn't believe this at all, whatever they may say. The world sees the rising money-loving financial star as someone to be envied. They plaster him on their magazine covers. They want to be seen with him at parties. They make movies about him. The apostle Paul, on the other hand, saw a man who is walking a tight-rope over a pit filled with sharp spikes, ready to be impaled. He saw a man who is wandering from the faith and exchanging God for material things.

Money is dangerous. If we really believed even half of what the Bible said about it, we would pray for those who are rich, rather than resenting them.

4. The Righteous Rich Are a Blessing

Being rich doesn't automatically make you a thief or a villain. Scripture presents many examples of rich people who were righteous and who used their wealth to bless those around them. Think of Job, Joseph, Zacchaeus, and Lydia.

Paul addressed the wealthy with these words in 1 Timothy 6:17-19:

> As for the rich in this present age, charge them not to be haughty, nor to set their hopes on the uncertainty of riches, but on God, who richly provides us with everything to enjoy. They are to do good, to be rich in good works, to be generous and ready to share, thus storing up treasure for themselves as a good foundation for the future, so that they may take hold of that which is truly life.

Two truths about being rich stand out in this passage. First, being rich is not inherently sinful. It doesn't prove someone a money worshipper, though envious people love to hurl this accusation. Paul did not say, "As for the rich in this age, tell them that they ought to be ashamed of themselves." Apparently, while it's not possible to serve both God and money (Matthew 6:24), it is possible to serve God *with* your money. Indeed, that is precisely what Paul told the rich to do.

Second, being rich brings an increased responsibility to be generous. Paul's counsel here echoes the saying of Jesus: "To whom much was given, of him much will be required" (Luke 12:48). God wants to use wealthy Christians as a blessing to the church and to the world.

5. Being Rich in This Age Is Astronomically Insignificant

Look at that 1 Timothy 6 passage again.

Notice that Paul addressed them as "those who are rich *in this present age*" (1 Timothy 6:17). The phrase "this present age" reflects the biblical teaching that human history is composed of two ages: this present age and the age to come (which Paul refers to as "the future" in verse 19). By using the phrase as he does here, Paul was implying a couple of things:

First, he implied that being rich in this present age doesn't guarantee you'll be rich in the age to come. If you're a rich person in this age, then the only way for you (or anyone else) to lay up a good foundation for riches in the age to come is to set your hope on God—that is, to grab hold of Christ with the kind of lively faith that proves itself by being generous (James 2:14-17; 1 John 3:17; Matthew 25:31-46).

Second, and more importantly, Paul implied that *being rich in this present age is infinitely less important than being rich in the age to come.* Get this, all who struggle with money envy! This is a fundamental truth that every Christian, rich or poor, needs to understand—namely, that being rich in this present age means almost nothing in light of eternity.

In the end, it's just not that big a deal.

Now don't misunderstand me. How we use our wealth is a huge deal. Indeed, it's such a reliable barometer of our faith in Christ that our eternal destiny could be revealed by it. Remember the goats in Matthew 25. Remember the rich man in Luke 16.

But when I say that being rich in this age means almost nothing, here's what I mean: being rich in this present age is nothing to be envious of, because in the end, this wealth is unbelievably short-lived. This present age is temporal, whereas the age to come is eternal (2 Corinthians 4:17-18).

In our envy, we look at our neighbor's designer clothes, luxury car, massive home, six-figure income, and European vacation and say to ourselves, "Now that's the life! He's really living!" But Paul said exactly the opposite. The life of the future—the eternal life of the age to come—is "that which is truly life" (1 Timothy 6:19). An "indestructible life" (Hebrews 7:16); a treasure that "neither moth nor rust destroys and thieves do not break in and steal" (Matthew 6:20); and "an inheritance that is imperishable, undefiled, and unfading, kept in heaven for you" (1 Peter 1:4)—*that* is truly life!

Compared to what's coming, this present age is breathtakingly short. It's an eye-blink's worth of prosperity. In Randy Alcorn's analogy, it's like a tiny dot compared to an unending line.[2] Envying your neighbor's lifestyle is an extreme form of tunnel vision; you're focusing on what goes on in the infinitesimal dot and ignoring the infinite line.

Compared to the momentary, ephemeral vapor of this present life (with its riches), "that which is truly life" will be unshakably firm, solid, and unending. That which is truly life belongs to the age to come, and we cannot yet see it in its fullness (2 Corinthians 5:7; 1 John 3:2). But according to Paul, all of us, rich or poor, can "take hold" of it now by faith. How? By setting our hope not "on the uncertainty of riches, but on God, who richly provides us with everything to enjoy" (1 Timothy 6:17).

So if you want to love your rich friend, don't envy her. If she has Christ, then encourage her to demonstrate it by blessing others with her wealth, and rejoice with her. If she doesn't have Christ, then she has nothing. No solid joys, no lasting pleasures, no foundation for the future. And that is not an enviable position.

Discussion Questions

- What are some of the things or options that you see other people enjoying and sometimes wish you had?

- Who are your peers? In what ways do the people around you affect your assumptions about your own standard of living?

- What are some scriptures to meditate on when we are worried about money (ours or our neighbor's)?

7

Borrowed Art:
The Envy of Creativity

*Since I became a novelist I have discovered that I am biased.
Either I think a new novel is worse than mine and I don't like
it, or I suspect it is better than my novels and I don't like it.*

UMBERTO ECO

All I ever wanted was to sing to God. He gave me that longing and then made me mute. Why? Tell me that. If he didn't want me to praise him with music, why implant the desire, like a lust in my body, and then deny me the talent?"

In this scene, Salieri the composer is confessing to the priest. This award-winning 1984 film, *Amadeus,* is a movie entirely about envy. It is about the obsession and hatred and deceitfulness of envy, through the eyes of one of the most envy-prone demographics in the world: artists.

Amadeus tells the story of Antonio Salieri's rivalrous relationship with Wolfgang Mozart, the genius child composer turned adult legend. At the opening of the movie, Salieri has just attempted suicide and is told encouragingly by the priest that confession is good for the soul.

Salieri hums several tunes, asking if the priest recognizes them. The priest politely, and with slight embarrassment, says that he doesn't.

07

"Can you remember no piece of mine?" asks Salieri in frustration. "I was the most famous composer in Europe. I wrote 40 operas alone." Finally, he hums a few bars of a very familiar piece. Anyone watching the movie recognizes it immediately, and so does the priest. He gets excited and finishes the tune.

"Yes, I know that! Oh, that's charming. I'm sorry; I didn't know you wrote that!"

Salieri is looking calmly at him. "I didn't," he says. "That was Mozart."

He then launches into the story of God's injustice. He tells how, as a little boy, he loved music more than anything, and prayed only for talent.

> While my father prayed earnestly to God to protect commerce, I would offer up secretly the proudest prayer a boy could think of: "Lord, make me a great composer. Let me celebrate your glory through music and be celebrated myself. Make me famous through the world, dear God. Make me immortal. After I die, let people speak my name forever with love for what I wrote. In return, I will give you my chastity, my industry, my deepest humility, every hour of my life. Amen."[1]

This very "humble" prayer, however, is not answered. Because while Salieri is enjoying a musical career as court composer for a monarch, Mozart suddenly appears on the scene. Mozart is instantly recognized as an exceptional musician. The only problem with Mozart is that he is inane, conceited, flirtatious, and has a laugh that could curdle milk.

Salieri has already heard the glory of one of Mozart's compositions, but he figures it must be a fluke. Then, one day, he is handed a folder of Mozart's works in progress.

They showed no corrections of any kind. Not one. He
had simply written down music already finished in his
head. Page after page of it as if he were just taking dic-
tation. And music, finished as no music is ever finished.
Displace one note and there would be diminishment.
Displace one phrase and the structure would fall...I
was staring through the cage of those meticulous ink
strokes—at an absolute beauty.[2]

Salieri describes his ensuing struggle to dethrone Mozart. He
immediately sees it for what it is: a battle cry against God himself.
After he understands that Mozart is a genius, he kneels before a cru-
cifix and prays the following prayer:

From now on we are enemies, you and I. Because you
choose for your instrument a boastful, lustful, smutty,
infantile boy and give me for reward only the ability to
recognize the incarnation. Because you are unjust, unfair,
unkind, I will block you, I swear it. I will hinder and
harm your creature on earth as far as I am able.[3]

Salieri's great plot is to anonymously commission a mass from
Mozart for money, then kill Mozart and play the mass as his own
work at Mozart's funeral.

This doesn't sound like the ultimate revenge, but to the insane
artist, it is perfect. "His funeral!" he rhapsodizes, years later, to the
now clearly disturbed priest.

Imagine it; the cathedral, all Vienna sitting there, his coffin, Mozart's little coffin in the middle, and then, in that
silence—music! A divine music bursts out over them
all. A great mass of death! Requiem mass for Wolfgang
Mozart, composed by his devoted friend, Antonio Salieri! Oh, what sublimity, what depth, what passion in

the music! Salieri has been touched by God at last. And
God is forced to listen! Powerless, powerless to stop it! I,
for once in the end, laughing at him![4]

We wonder to ourselves, is this really what Salieri wants? Would
it really satisfy him, to be known for creating one piece that was
really genius? Would that do it for him, knowing that it was a lie?

None of that matters to the insane musician. For Salieri, revenge
against God would be accomplished simply by falsely taking back
glory that he believes God took from him and gave to an imbecile.

In the end, Salieri fails in his bizarre plotting—Mozart dies too
soon. The insane Salieri is wheeled away at the end of the movie,
telling the shaken priest and all the others in the asylum that he is
the patron saint of mediocrities.

"I absolve you…I absolve you…I absolve you all."

Pretend Games and the Nature of the Universe

Art is one of mankind's favorite idolatries. There's music, televi-
sion, film, theater, painting, sculpture, architecture, graphics, and
the written word, and we're eating it all up. We live in a world that
places an almost mythical importance on art. We believe that even
when we get rid of any allegiance to a knowable higher power, art
is so emotive and lovely and glorious that it can be our replacement
source of meaning.

The old false gods had priests or oracles or witch doctors. Now
we have artists.

What is it about art that makes us feel so close to touching the
meaning of the universe? What is it about these experiences—at a
gallery or a music venue or in a library—that gives us the sensation
of brushing our fingers against the outer door of glory itself?

I think it's because of the need for story that God has built into us.
Have you ever noticed what happens when you leave children alone

together for more than about five minutes? They start to play. And what do they start to play, assuming there's no screen in the room?

They make up and act out stories.

When my sisters and I were young and outnumbered the boys five to two, we played two games: "Love" and "House." Very occasionally we played "Journey," all of us piled high on a wagon with a lot of wooden chairs on top, with Father "away at war" and Mother, played by my sister Sophie, constantly halting proceedings to give birth.

The love stories had predictable themes. Some kind of bad guy was usually chasing a damsel around, and there was a good guy who was supposed to come in and do battle against the bad guy to rescue her and marry her under the dogwood tree in the front yard. Or there were two workers in a fancy kitchen who connected while shaking out the same rug, under the jealous and watchful eye of the Evil Boss, and they had to run away together.

We thought our stories had never been thought of by anyone else. But it turned out, all the neighborhood kids were doing the same thing.

The boys who lived two houses over were playing their own pretend games, except all of theirs had a different central theme: a battle between good and evil. They were cops chasing bad guys or superheroes fighting off villains, or Harry Potter rising up to destroy Lord Voldemort.

Collaborations between these two houses were impossible. The boys, generally preferred to play alone, bored by our attempts to introduce romantic side plots.

But it is interesting to me to note that in general, girls play romance and boys play war. And what kind of plot would you say redemptive history is? If you had to identify a "type" for the great drama of rebellion, fall, expulsion, pursuit, ongoing conflict, reconcilement, and final triumph that we are currently living through?

It's a romance. It's a war.

Artists Are Warriors

Art tells stories. That's what it's for. This is true of music and novels and movies and dances and paintings and sculptures and poems. Good art tells stories well. Bad art tells stories badly. But all of it tells a story of some kind. These art stories are either true or they are lies—or some combination of the two.

We also know that God is telling a story and that all of us are characters in this story. He's been telling it for many thousands of years, and he will continue to tell it until his master story is complete.

So this brings us to a sober conclusion. If art is storytelling, and if the nature of the universe is a story, then artists are actually warriors. If artists are warriors, and if God is in the middle of a great battle against evil, then all of these warriors are fighting on one of two sides.

Surely this puts the question of art envy into another perspective. If we are all warriors, then we are fighting well or badly, depending on the quality of our craft. This means that when we see another artist who fights better than we do by telling better stories with more brilliance, more understanding, and more talent, then we have one of two battle plans.

If they are telling lies with their art (such as "sex is the source of meaning" or "reality is chaos"), then we should oppose them with our humble talents in any way we can. Will we do this by openly calling them out? Perhaps. But more importantly, we will do this by telling true stories. We'll tell them as often and as well as we can. Our talents will limit us—what are we, anyway, except foot soldiers?—but we must march, and we must attack with all the strength of our pens and guitars and paintbrushes. God is the General.

We ask him for help, but not the way Salieri did it. He said, in essence, "God, give me talent and glory, and in return I will give you my chastity." We say, "God, use the tool, however blunt it is. Help me to take responsibility to work with what you have given me. Let me not cower in the fight, and let me never think that my talent does anything for the kingdom but what you ordain."

And what about when we see another warrior on our team who fights harder, stronger, faster, and better than we ever could? Do we despair because we are foot soldiers instead of great cavalrymen? No! We rejoice! That other warrior is *on our side*. We should cheer to see any stroke against the enemy made by any hand.

If we can't rejoice at genuine strokes of beauty wielded against our satanic enemies, then we are obviously blind to the battle. We obviously don't love the General or the thing he fights for, if we begrudge points scored by people on our own team. Obviously, in moments of creative envy, we are only seeing one thing: the eyes of men. We have forgotten the spiritual realm altogether.

This is the way defectors are made.

Three Things We Know About Art from Scripture

We have to saturate our minds in Scripture in order to keep our eyes open to the spiritual nature of what we're doing in the creative world.

1. God Is the Original Artist

Let's start with the obvious: God created everything.

We get to watch in absentia, our imaginations tantalized, as we read the story in Genesis 1. God said, "Let there be light" (verse 3). He called the light "Day" and the darkness "Night" (verse 5). Yes, as part of some mysterious creative process he invented the phenomenon that we call light. Later he invented he sun, along with the lesser lights that rule the night—thinking up, along with those wonders, the processes we call photosynthesis, photography, photochemical reaction, photoemission, and photocells. He invented light; apparently in some other sense he *is* light (John 1:4-9; 8:12; 9:5).

God's creative energy expanded to the invention of stumbling fawns, pulsing veins, peonies exploding into bloom, whales digesting invisible living things, the moon as reflector, and the shocking thing that can happen to dried corn kernels when you heat them.

In fact, every common and ordinary thing we observe in God's green world—observable and repeatable—is a resounding chorus of artistic genius. The art is so astounding, such consistently good art, that there are huge branches of human study devoted to the observation, analysis, and exploration of it. We call these the sciences. Johannes Kepler, one of the world's greatest scientists, referred to the sciences as the process of "thinking God's thoughts after him."[5]

This is exactly what art amounts to. What we do is take material left here by the master Artist and remix it. That's all we can do.

We take the plotlines of God's story, collected and reimagined into fictional stories. We take meaning injected into our hearts and languages by the Word made flesh and express it as well as we can in poetry and prose. We take the varying wavelengths of sound, with numbers already built into reality by an orderly God, and filter them together to make music. We act out stories on the stage, using muscles in faces that God designed aesthetically. We splash truth and beauty onto canvasses, in colors that he dreamed up, and etch it into stones that he mixed and poured already. Even our best work can only remind others of something that God has already painted or carved.

2. God Commissions Art

Even with the knowledge that our art is a borrowed glory, we can know that God smiles on the endeavor. He is a supporter of the arts. The first commissioner of art recorded in Scripture, in fact, was God himself.

In Exodus, God gave detailed instructions for the creation of his tabernacle, as well as furniture to fill it, ornamentation to decorate it, the ark of the covenant to be housed in it, perfume and incense to scent it, and clothing for his priests to wear when entering it. Then God told Moses that not only was God the commissioner, but he was also the one who would make it possible for the talent to meet the challenge:

> The LORD said to Moses, "See, I have called by name Bezalel the son of Uri, son of Hur, of the tribe of Judah, and I have filled him with the Spirit of God, with ability and intelligence, with knowledge and all craftsmanship, to devise artistic designs, to work in gold, silver, and bronze, in cutting stones for setting, and in carving wood, to work in every craft. And behold, I have appointed with him Oholiab, the son of Ahisamach, of the tribe of Dan. And I have given to all able men ability, that they may make all that I have commanded you… According to all that I have commanded you, they shall do" (Exodus 31:1-6,11).

I like to imagine the excitement of the artisans when the orders came down for this project. After all, I'm sure they've loved this kind of work for a very long time. Perhaps they had been doing it wherever they could for years, the way so many artists do—holding day jobs just so they can head to the backyard at the end of the day and work the craft.

They didn't know that they'd eventually get this life-changing commission. They only knew that they loved to devise, to cut stones, to create. When they did these things, they felt the Lord's pleasure. And now they found that they were going to be set loose to do what they loved to do on the most important job they would ever have.

God, the original artist, has shown himself to be interested in beauty. If he weren't, he wouldn't have wasted time on butterflies.

He also wouldn't have sent the Holy Spirit on purpose to enable these artisans to make beautiful things for his temple.

Jesus, the God-man who walked among us, also put his hand to the work of an artist—storytelling. In obedience to his Father, he told stories. He told stories that made such a mark on his audience that light itself spread into the world through the retelling of the stories.

Jesus smiled on the seemingly frivolous use of an alabaster flask of fragrant oil (Luke 7:36-49), took time to restore sight to men who were unable to look upon the beauty of his world (Matthew 9:27-30; 15:30-31; Mark 8:22-25; Mark 10:46-52), and unstopped the ears of the deaf until they could hear the words of a book (Isaiah 29:18).

Art was a vehicle for truth with the God-man, who wasted no word or moment. Even with his life's purpose constantly in mind, it seems that he found the stories worth telling, the sight worth restoring, and the perfume worth pouring.

And let's not forget one of the great works of art that God inspired and directed: the compiled books of the Bible. In this great work, we find poetry like the following:

> Three things are too wonderful for me;
>   four I do not understand:
> the way of an eagle in the sky,
>   the way of a serpent on a rock,
> the way of a ship on the high seas,
>   and the way of a man with a virgin…
> Under three things the earth trembles;
>   under four it cannot bear up:
> a slave when he becomes king,
>   and a fool when he is filled with food;
> an unloved woman when she gets a husband,

and a maidservant when she displaces her mistress
(Proverbs 30:18-19,21-23).

God in his sovereignty had every word of this fanciful and wise juxtaposition between wild nature and human nature. He thought it was worthwhile that a copy of these lines made it from the poet's pen, through the passing of time, to the leather-bound collections we hold in our hands now.

God the artist is also a commissioner of art.

3. God Gives the "Talents," but We Are Responsible for How We Use Them

Let's go back to one of those stories Jesus told to remind our-selves of something we've established already. If beauty and mean-ing are, as we've been discussing, real values in God's economy, then this means that there is glory in the ability to produce these things.

It's particularly convenient that one of the units of money used in Jesus's time was called a *talent*. I like to read this particular para-ble with another meaning in mind (paragraphs added):

> [The kingdom of heaven] will be like a man going on a journey, who called his servants and entrusted to them his property. To one he gave five talents, to another two, to another one, to each according to his ability. Then he went away.
>
> He who had received the five talents went at once and traded with them, and he made five talents more. So also he who had the two talents made two talents more. But he who had received the one talent went and dug in the ground and hid his master's money.
>
> Now after a long time the master of those servants came and settled accounts with them. And he who had

received the five talents came forward, bringing five talents more, saying, "Master, you delivered to me five talents; here I have made five talents more." His master said to him, "Well done, good and faithful servant. You have been faithful over a little; I will set you over much. Enter into the joy of your master." And he also who had the two talents came forward, saying, "Master, you delivered to me two talents; here I have made two talents more." His master said to him, "Well done, good and faithful servant. You have been faithful over a little; I will set you over much. Enter into the joy of your master."

He also who had received the one talent came forward, saying, "Master, I knew you to be a hard man, reaping where you did not sow, and gathering where you scattered no seed, so I was afraid, and I went and hid your talent in the ground. Here, you have what is yours."

But his master answered him, "You wicked and slothful servant! You knew that I reap where I have not sown and gather where I scattered no seed? Then you ought to have invested my money with the bankers, and at my coming I should have received what was my own with interest. So take the talent from him and give it to him who has the ten talents. For to everyone who has will more be given, and he will have an abundance. But from the one who has not, even what he has will be taken away" (Matthew 25:14-29).

Now in the metaphor of this story, think of the Master's lent money in terms of artistic giftings, or "talents." One person gets ten. Another gets five. Somebody gets just one.

Imagine your own reaction to the disbursement of these borrowed glories. You're an aspiring actor who's been given the ability to do one thing really well: dramatic monologue. You dream of playing Hamlet. Your classmate in drama school, however, seems to have five talents to your one. He can do straight drama, comedy, improv, and slapstick—plus he can sing.

They give Hamlet to him.

But then imagine that Matt Damon is at your school too. He can do all those things, but he also writes—he writes himself a part straight into Hollywood and also possesses the skill and the build to be an action star, a dramatic film actor, and even to do comedy on occasion.

As he shoots up and away, fulfilling all the glorious potential represented by his ten talents, you languish in an art school classroom. Soon, you find that you just can't do it anymore. Your one talent isn't worth all this risk and pain. You stop auditioning for roles. You quit art school. You get more and more bitter as you pursue your new career choice of accounting. Eventually you stop going to plays. You avoid movies that star Matt Damon. You stop reading scripts of any kind, and you behave satirically when anyone brings up the fact that you used to go to art school.

You've buried your talent in the ground. The talent, which may at least have been used to enhance your enjoyment of excellent work, is used for nothing but bringing forth a crop of bitterness.

Someday, you'll be asked to justify the fruit you produced with the seed that was your one talent. You point to the five-talent guy and say, "Well, I didn't produce; I couldn't. If I'd had what he has, I could have really done something. I figured it wasn't worthwhile to cultivate this one little seed. I put it in a box though; you can have it back…"

You'll know in that day what is really true. Your envy is no excuse, and you have made yourself into the kind of person who would have done no better with five talents than you have done with one. To him who has, more will be given. To him who doesn't have, even what he has will be taken away.

The attitude of the artist-warrior is everything.

Take stock of what you have been given. Call yourself to account for it. Look around you at the stories being told by the artists in your life. Are the stories true? Rejoice in the talent that God has spread among his people. Are the stories false? Combat the falsehood, and pray for the one who uses his art to tell falsehoods.

Remember what love does, according to 1 Corinthians 13—it "does not rejoice at wrongdoing but rejoices with the truth" (verse 6). Love "bears all things, believes all things, hopes all things, endures all things" (verse 7). This means that when you witness the artistic output of those around you, you must pray for a heart that rejoices with the truth. You want a default setting that jumps to find good things in what people are making and feels sorrow to see lies being told or art done badly. The same default setting is quick to collaborate, wishing to bear all things, believe all things, hope all things, and endure all things.

And as an artist, responsible for the lens through which you view the world, remember this exhortation from Paul:

> Whatever is true, whatever is honorable, whatever is just, whatever is pure, whatever is lovely, whatever is commendable, if there is any excellence, if there is anything worthy of praise, think about these things (Philippians 4:8).

We are, after all, only imitators of the great Artist, thinking his thoughts after him. When we saturate our minds with Scripture, the truths we tell will be richer, purer, lovelier, more commendable, and more excellent. And they will be told as unto God—the great commissioner to whom we will one day give account for our use of the talents.

There's no room for envy in this story.

Discussion Questions

- Salieri is a great example of an envious artist who knows that his complaint is against God. Can you think of other examples of art envy in literature or real life?

- Art is storytelling, which means that art is a way of fighting in the battle between good and evil. Have you ever seen or listened to a piece of art that was skillfully done but telling lies?

- Can you see any creative area where you know you've been given one "talent," but somebody else has been given five or ten? Is there any area in which you feel you've been given a full portion of "talent," and others have resented you for it?

- What are some ways you could see squandering your "talent" on selfish gains instead of spending it on the fight between good and evil?

8

Borrowed Tasks: The Envy of Competence and Control

Not that we are competent in ourselves to claim anything for ourselves, but our competence comes from God. He has made us competent as ministers of a new covenant—not of the letter but of the Spirit; for the letter kills, but the Spirit gives life.

2 CORINTHIANS 3:5-6 NIV

When I was young, I had a friend who was very serious. She wasn't the girl who sat out of fun games and ran to tell parents when you did something you weren't supposed to, and she wasn't the girl who fretted and stressed about getting the best possible grade. In fact, she wasn't greatly emotional about anything. She was serene, rather.

She knew how things were supposed to be done, and she was happy to do them herself, quietly. She wasn't afraid of work, and she wasn't particularly shy. She was neither dramatic nor impersonal, but she was definitely a doer, and she was efficient.

I remember feeling a mixture of respect and pity for her back then. It was wonderful that she was so measured, so *right* all the time. Naturally, that inspired a sort of childish awe in me. But I felt pity for anyone who did not feel things as deeply as I felt them. I believed that she was coming up short in the emotional spectrum if she didn't cry during movies and never had crushes. Surely there were a great many experiences that she was missing out on. For me, experiences had very much to do with emotional displays. My crushes, my passions, my elaborate daydreams, my creative enterprises—they all had to do with feeling.

They had nothing to do with productivity.

We went in different directions as children. Our families fell out of touch, and there were many formative years during which we never saw one another. Later, though, we came back into contact. I found her to be a more productive, more mature version of her childhood self. She was not cold, but she was methodical. She was not frenzied, but she was busy. She had goals, but they were not numerical—they had to do with tasks and people.

Her life had been steady, serene, and smooth. She'd been governed by principle, and the things she believed in, she appeared to have acted on. Now she was reaping the fruit of good, solid relationships; a good, solid job; and a good, solid heart.

She was about to get married—to someone whom all the flighty, pretty girls had probably wanted. And I knew that there had been nothing flashy in her to attract this godly young man—it was all that quiet steadiness of character. She told me that she hadn't even been sure she wanted to get married. She rather preferred the life she had and was not one to welcome change.

It was the first time a single girl said something like that to me, and I believed her.

I, in the meantime, had wasted those years. These were the years of open rebellion for me—when thought reaping action reaping habit reaping character had produced chaos and despair in my own life. The comparison between us became only more painful over time, perhaps as I began to long for the virtue of faithfulness and to see how hard it was going to be for me to learn.

The parallels were only too clear. We were both homeschooled, both churched, both from large families with fathers who hugged us.

But I was a college graduate who was apparently unemployable. I had been pursued by men, but none of them were what I saw as marriageable. Having teased a couple of them, I now felt cheap and used up. I had been the sort of person who accepted multiple invitations on a Friday night so that I could freely leave one place and go to another if I wasn't having fun. A flaky person and something of a liar, I could not be relied on to show up to things or to be satisfied with a job for more than three months.

Now, some of what I was envying in my friend was godliness—which I recognized both before and after my conversion. But the thing that I really recognized in her and wanted was her quiet ability to get things done. She was *competent*. She was in control of her life, and whether she was trusting in the Holy Spirit for that or trusting herself, I didn't know or care.

A year or two after we became friends again, I had lost none of my respect for her, but I began to feel that I was being dismissed. I was growing, slowly, but it had become impossible for me to resist comparing her good fruit with the rotten stuff I was having to pick, bag up, and throw out. And then there was this uncomfortable feeling that she had identified my inferiority. She was not the sort to rub things in my face or be openly disrespectful, but I could not help but see that she, in her quiet way, didn't consider us equals.

No one—remember what C.S. Lewis said—feels the need to say, "I'm just as good as you," unless they aren't. One day I found myself daydreaming about having that specific conversation with her, and I knew I was in deep spiritual trouble.

This is what I wanted to say to her, to hear her acknowledge and admit out loud: that she couldn't exactly explain why her life was so smooth. I wanted to walk her through all the blessings she'd been given—her genes, her training, her natural personality, her opportunities, and her unexpected connections—and I wanted her to admit that in each of these things God could have chosen to give her a different lot. She could have been a mess instead of a clean, quietly humming machine, meeting deadlines and planning her meals a week in advance.

She could have been (and let's be honest, this is what I really wanted her to know) *like me.*

When I realized soon after her marriage that I had built up a store of resentment in my heart toward her, I didn't know what to do about it. I certainly hadn't identified it for what it was. Eventually we had a conversation—stilted and not immediately to the point—where I tried to acknowledge the rift between us, and I think we both came away confused for a time. It took a few years more of the Lord working in my heart, privately, before I could begin to name and address my actual sin against her.

And it wasn't until I found my heart warm toward her again and communication had been generally reestablished that I was able to look back and use the word *envy.* Aah. That was the problem. That's what was going on.

Nobody who says, "I'm just as good as you" actually believes it.

"Give Me an Occupation, Miss Dashwood, or I Shall Run Mad"

We talked about money earlier. And often, people who work hard and do something well have more money. But the money is not the mainly enviable thing, as far as my experience goes. It's the job itself that I am more likely to want.

This is my generation, see. In my generation, you don't just get a job and go to work and get paid and support your family. You are *fulfilled* or *unfulfilled.* You have to go into a career that is *relevant* and *enriching.* People I'm connected to on LinkedIn have job titles like "environmental internet researcher," "digital media consultant," "CEO/storyteller," "spiritual innovator," and "street marketer." I'm not sure what any of these people do, but it sure sounds exciting.

Maybe I'm wrong, but it seems like people used to just be called a teacher, farmer, salesman, or preacher. They worked for money, and then they went home and ate dinner.

Then again, I don't remember very far back.

I can look at my life now and see that this unreasonable expectation—"you can do anything and be anything you want"—was responsible for many dumb moves on my part. I would have spent my time better, learning how to just do a good job at something instead of scrambling to find the one job that would exactly suit my strengths and interests, the job that would require nothing uncomfortable of me and deliver a nice living wage.

Instead, I found myself dumped out of college and into the job market in 2008. Later, I found out that this had been the worst time in many decades for a person to be entering the job market. Many of my friends struggled, and many of them, I'm sure, couldn't understand why they were struggling. We all sort of expected to walk out of school with a diploma and get offered $50K a year, just for being naturally fantastic.

It was a painful and rude awakening to realize that I had not necessarily made my educational decisions based on any understanding of the job market. I quickly decided that I would give a great deal to go back and come out of school with the technical training to *do* something, like nurse somebody or teach math. Instead, I had been trained to read the classics and write news stories—something that no one seemed to want to pay me for.

Many of my friends had a more practical, diligent bent than I. They were of above-average intelligence too. Among them, ten years later, I now know doctors, lab researchers, PhDs, editors, and accountants. They run the full range between right and left brains, but the presiding theme seems to be a healthy dose of diligence. They had a goal, most of them, and they followed through until that goal was accomplished.

I, in the meantime, have worked the following jobs since freshman year of college: I was a swim instructor, an assistant teacher, a session singer, doughnut shop manager, waitress in three different restaurants, hostess in one restaurant, office assistant to a real-estate appraiser, perfume saleslady, internet music blogger, writer for the school paper, assistant writer for a set of self-help books, interim teacher, au pair, grad student, and insurance salesperson. I had none of these jobs for more than six months or so.

This is what you call floundering.

I stayed at each of these jobs just long enough to be sure I didn't want to try very hard at them. Rather than being interested in competence, I was interested in having a job that was respectable. I wanted to be able to tell people about my job without flinching. It never occurred to me that I should just find a gap and stick around long enough to plug it.

If You Can't Run with the Big Dogs...

There is a danger that comes with being competent as well. There is a danger that comes when you are running full speed ahead, enjoying the pumping of your own legs and the joy of efficiency, and you look back to see people struggling behind you.

You begin to be impatient. There isn't time for them to be slow! Why can't they simply move, pumping their legs like you do? Don't they understand how muscles work? Don't they *want* to be fast?

I remember the first time I looked around me and noticed that competence had crept into my life. I had finally gotten a job that lined up with my skill set—I was the editor of a small weekly newspaper. My journalism major was being put to good use, and I was busy and had a pleasant feeling of fulfilling a real need.

I worked constantly that first year. It seemed like the deadlines never quit coming. We didn't have much staff, so I was working with mainly freelancers. I had never worked in news and didn't know the county very well. I had never been to a city council meeting, a board of education meeting, a commissioner's meeting. I had never been in a courtroom. I didn't know the county mayors, the city mayors, the sheriff, or the head of the local Lions Club. All of that soon changed.

My husband and I bought a house and did some renovations a few years after we got married. I experienced the totally pure joy of making tea with my own pot and cooking meals. Mopping on Saturdays. Standing at my own sink with my own sudsy pot in my hands. Putting clothes in a washing machine and not letting them pile up. It was almost a sensual pleasure, really—keeping a home.

I started running again, as I used to. My husband and I started having people over to dinner. I started bringing dishes to the church potluck. I painted my office on my own time, just because it needed it. I learned how simple it can be to simply show up for things (on time!), and started making myself more available for ministry opportunities. We found that we were no longer watching much TV, because the hours were simply being used in other ways.

But something else began to happen simultaneously. It wasn't long after I got this job, populated my kitchen, and started dotting the i's and crossing the t's that it started.

I began to get impatient with incompetence.

I became upset that people would turn things in with mistakes in them. (Had I forgotten that my job title was "Editor"?) I felt a gentle condescension toward the people in town who never cooked at home, who never exercised or read books. I developed a sort of

eye-rolling impatience toward my husband, who did not appreci-
ate the importance of our "just for looks" hand towel.

There's something about having a job to get done, I guess. Something about running fast and lining up ducks makes you snappy
about people who are slow, about ducks that get out of line. And it
is inexcusable for anyone, but for me it is doubly inexcusable. Why?
Because so shortly ago, I was the one who was stumbling, limping,
and crawling up the road. I was the duck out of line.

After years of wishing that all the efficient people would slow
down just a little and help me with my mess, I had no time for
messes. After years of feeling outraged when people correctly
deemed themselves more diligent and professional, I instantly forgot about my outrage when the time came. It took no time at all for
me to begin thinking in terms of "if you can't run with the big dogs,
then stay on the porch."

Of course, all of this was before I had my first child.

Since then? I cannot comment.

Four Things We Know About Competence from Scripture

The best way for us to get a healthy view of competence is by
looking at the truth of God's Word.

1. God Is the Ultimate Competence

The competence of God should silence us, with our professor-
ships, factories, and coupon drawers. We got nothin'.

Paul made this clear in his second letter to the Corinthians. "Not
that we are competent in ourselves to claim anything for ourselves," he
writes, "but our competence comes from God. He has made us competent as ministers of a new covenant—not of the letter but of the Spirit;
for the letter kills, but the Spirit gives life" (2 Corinthians 3:5-6 NIV).

It might be impressive when you find a man who knows how to operate on a human heart, how to fix a carburetor, and how to play the cello. It might be dazzling to see a woman who understands property value and can show three houses in the same afternoon, then sit down and whip out a child's garment at a sewing machine. But none of our abilities originates with ourselves, and none of them holds a candle to the gloriously competent one.

God expressed this idea almost sarcastically during a debate with Job and his foolish friends; the same debate over their relative levels of wisdom that we looked at a few chapters ago gets carried into a new topic. Let's allow his words in Job 38:4-13 to speak for themselves:

> Where were you when I laid the foundation of the earth?
>   Tell me, if you have understanding.
> Who determined its measurements—surely you know!
>   Or who stretched the line upon it?
> On what were its bases sunk,
>   or who laid its cornerstone,
> when the morning stars sang together
>   and all the sons of God shouted for joy?
> Or who shut in the sea with doors
>   when it burst out from the womb,
> when I made clouds its garment
>   and thick darkness its swaddling band,
> and prescribed limits for it
>   and set bars and doors,
> and said, "Thus far shall you come, and no farther,
>   and here shall your proud waves be stayed"?
> Have you commanded the morning since your days began,
>   and caused the dawn to know its place,
> that it might take hold of the skirts of the earth,
>   and the wicked be shaken out of it?

He goes on. God had plenty to say about his utterly exclusive abilities. Finally, as we saw earlier, Job, who was quieted along with his friends, responded simply, "Behold, I am of small account; what shall I answer you? I lay my hand on my mouth" (Job 40:4).

Later he acknowledged, "I know that you can do all things, and that no purpose of yours can be thwarted" (Job 42:2).

This can't be said of anyone else in the universe.

2. The Poor in Spirit Are Blessed

We've all known a person who seemed to simply always be in a state of emergency. They seem to have too many kids, not enough house, a car that is always breaking down, and a job that is too much for them. They may not be very helpful in the community, and they are unlikely to take on extra projects at work because they have so much to handle in their own lives. They are often aware of this and likely feel the pain of knowing that they are not one of the "doers."

But these people are in a uniquely advantaged position; they have an excellent vantage point from which to become one of those whom Jesus called "poor in spirit."

"Blessed are the poor in spirit," said Jesus, "for theirs is the kingdom of heaven" (Matthew 5:3).

Those who are overwhelmed and humbled by circumstance should remember that Jesus did not orient the kingdom of heaven around the doers. If so, the Pharisees would have been arranged in a little line and marched straight up to the mercy seat (or what they would have called the "get what you've earned" seat). The kingdom of heaven is oriented toward the last, not the first.

But are those who are "poor in spirit" people who constantly writhe under dishonor or charity? Are they gnashing their teeth against those around them who don't appear to struggle? No. If so, they can no longer be called poor in spirit.

Humility is a key factor in the character of those who are truly poor in spirit. They know that they are unable to earn God's favor by performing well. They know that they struggle, and they are spiritually insightful enough not to confuse efficiency with righteous dependence on the blood of Christ. Their response is to call out for help, not to shake their fists.

Jesus is not glorifying ineptitude or self-pity when he blesses the poor in spirit. He is commending the humble people, the people who see their weakness clearly. And like a rich man struggles to get through the eye of a needle, a doer usually struggles to see his own weakness.

3. We Are Called to Work as unto the Lord

It is honorable to God to be a hard worker, to manage your life well, and to be skilled. A man who can work a full-time job to feed his family, doing such a great job that they give him extra projects, and still get home in time to eat with them brings glory to God—if he does it in worship. A woman who can serve the PTA, the ladies' ministry, and the Rotary Club while running a small business and cooking organic meals brings glory to God—if she does it in worship.

Colossians 3:23 commands us well: "Whatever you do, work heartily, as for the Lord and not for men." That online class, job, or PTA meeting is not something you just have to do for you, and it's not something you do primarily for your boss or for the local school. You do it for the Lord. Interestingly, though, it's the men and women around you who benefit from your work. God doesn't need your productivity, but he can often use it to provide for others.

There are all kinds of dangers in being a doer, and the word is not often used in a positive sense in Christian circles. But a person who actually acts, instead of standing around and talking about it, is lauded in Scripture. We could bring dozens of examples to play in the spiritual realm. ("Be doers of the word, and not hearers only," advises James 1:22.) But Proverbs 14:23 addresses physical work specifically: "In all toil there is profit," it says, "but mere talk tends only to poverty."

First Thessalonians 4:11-12 has solid advice for the Christian who is constantly making himself a burden on those around him: "Aspire to live quietly, and to mind your own affairs, and to work with your hands, as we instructed you, so that you may walk properly before outsiders and be dependent on no one."

This is not a call for church members to avoid ever being in one another's debt or showing weakness or asking for help. On the contrary, we see myriad examples in the New Testament of men and women sharing one another's burdens and giving freely to those in need (Acts 2:42-47; 4:32-37). Rather, these verses communicate *responsibility*. Let us be responsible for our own diligence within the framework of our abilities and our sphere.

4. Our Competence Is Limited to Our Area of Assignment

Your job is to do your job, great or small, and do it to the best of your God-given ability. It's not to check out your neighbor's assignment. It's certainly not to burn inwardly because somebody you know is accomplishing more in his sphere than you are in yours.

What are you good at? Work to get better. What task do you see near you that needs doing? Do it. Don't waste your time reaching over, getting your fingers tangled up in your neighbor's task. Don't waste your time comparing his weed patch to your own.

Remember the parable of the vineyard workers in Matthew 20:1-16 (paragraphs added):

> The kingdom of heaven is like a master of a house who went out early in the morning to hire laborers for his

vineyard. After agreeing with the laborers for a denarius a day, he sent them into his vineyard.

And going out about the third hour he saw others standing idle in the marketplace, and to them he said, "You go into the vineyard too, and whatever is right I will give you." So they went. Going out again about the sixth hour and the ninth hour, he did the same. And about the eleventh hour he went out and found others standing. And he said to them, "Why do you stand here idle all day?" They said to him, "Because no one has hired us." He said to them, "You go into the vineyard too."

And when evening came, the owner of the vineyard said to his foreman, "Call the laborers and pay them their wages, beginning with the last, up to the first." And when those hired about the eleventh hour came, each of them received a denarius. Now when those hired first came, they thought they would receive more, but each of them also received a denarius.

And on receiving it they grumbled at the master of the house, saying, "These last worked only one hour, and you have made them equal to us who have borne the burden of the day and the scorching heat." But he replied to one of them, "Friend, I am doing you no wrong. Did you not agree with me for a denarius? Take what belongs to you and go. I choose to give to this last worker as I give to you. Am I not allowed to do what I choose with what belongs to me? Or do you begrudge my generosity?" So the last will be first, and the first last.

God has put you in the field in a certain row and made agreements with you about the terms of your employment. Looking over into the next row is never going to do anybody any good. Keep to your task. Do it with all your might, and be joyful in your work. Be grateful for the reward that he's promised. And don't even begin to imagine that those tasks are somehow setting you up to be independent of the loving Taskmaster.

This is yet another borrowed glory, friends. Even your obedience was given to you.

Discussion Questions

- How do you handle it when you feel incompetent?

- How do you handle it when you encounter someone who is uber-competent?

- Do you think that envy and laziness ever go together? Why or why not?

- You've likely heard the phrase "hoe your own row" to reference the idea of minding your own business and leaving others to mind theirs. Do you think this is a biblical idea? Why or why not?

9

Borrowed Trinity: The Envy of Relationship

Jesus said to him, "I am the way, and the truth, and the life. No one comes to the Father except through me. If you had known me, you would have known my Father also. From now on you do know him and have seen him."

JOHN 14:6-7

He was 18 months old when his mother died. Cancer took her bones.

Sam was the last of her children. All over the country, she had other families by other fathers that she'd begun and then abandoned to start a new life. After Sam's mother died, his father left Sam and his siblings in an orphanage and fled the country.

The people who ran this orphanage believed that the only thing children needed instilled in them was fear. They told Sam regularly that he was going to hell, and he remembers being locked out of the orphanage doors with a man outside instructed to jump out and scare him.

Eventually his mother's brother came to the orphanage and got the kids. He didn't adopt them, but he did take them home. At his house, there was more abuse and dysfunction. Sam, who knew he was going to hell no matter what he did, began to act out. By the time he was a preteen, one of his dad's brothers offered to take him in since he'd grown to be such a handful. This man, a veterinarian who kept a kind, Christian home, had three other sons. This is the man who eventually formally adopted Sam.

Sam came into the family with his fists up.

One of his new brothers, Jimmy, was just a few years older than Sam. Jimmy was the perfect son. He was easygoing, studious, and liked by all. He had a special relationship with his father already. Sam shadowed Jimmy through the upper grades. Everywhere he went, he was known to others as Jimmy's brother.

The problem was that he didn't act like Jimmy's brother.

Sam lied compulsively, for one thing. He would look his new family members in the eye and tell them he hadn't done something that they had just watched him do—*when he knew that they had just watched him do it*. Later, he was arrested for stealing from a local store that he worked in; he'd been casually taking things home at the end of the workday. When they caught him, he simply shrugged.

He behaved as if nothing bothered him—but growing in his heart was a seething, hot rage. It was directed toward the world in general, but a special slice of it was reserved for Jimmy. Jimmy, with his easy manner, who had been in this family and community the whole time, who bore the marks of a lifetime of safety and security. Jimmy, who went on a hunting trip alone with his own father every year. Jimmy, who told his mom "I love you" every day before leaving the house. All of Jimmy's relationships were in order. People trusted him and loved him. There were people whom he loved and trusted.

Sam had never had that. Even now in his adopted status, time couldn't be reversed. He had lost the good years. He was ruined now. His new family looked askance at him, left him out—he could feel it. He'd never be one of them.

Once, Sam insisted on coming along for the father-son hunting trip with Jimmy and Dad. But once he had forced his point and the three of them were in the woods, he found himself unable to enjoy it. He complained and cussed. He knew they didn't want him along—and he wanted to make sure they knew it too. Eventually he ended up falling asleep in the blind, wasting a $200 gear rental.

As a young adult, Sam fell hard for drugs and the wild homosexual community of the 1980s. He lived what felt like a hundred lifetimes. He had eight or ten different careers. He was cut off, one by one, by all his adopted siblings as his abusive behavior became increasingly difficult to handle.

Only one brother continued to talk to him—Jimmy.

Sam would occasionally fly into rages and text or call Jimmy out of the blue, leaving expletive-laden messages of hatred. Then, the next time he called he would be a different person. Every year or so, Sam called to hurl abuses at Jimmy and insist again that a relationship would be impossible until Jimmy affirmed his gay lifestyle. Jimmy, a Christian, said only that he felt it would be better if they talked about other things.

Beneath the rocky ups and downs of the relationship was one bitter fact that Sam could never forget.

God had given Jimmy a family. First, he had given Jimmy a family of origin, and then he had given him another family of his own with a wife and kids. He'd made him the sort of person who plays nice with others, who has lots of good friends and healthy relationships. He'd even made Jimmy the sort of person who takes a beating from his adopted brother/cousin and keeps answering the phone.

In short, Sam could never forgive Jimmy for having a father. And he could never forgive God for giving him one.

The Need to Be Inside

Yesterday I went to our local gym. It was the day after Thanksgiving, and it was cold. We have only one gym in our town, only one that has full sets of free weights and is open to the public. It's in a small, glass-front building in a strip mall, and though not very big, it has the necessary things: a few working treadmills, lots of mirrors, a largish lifting area, and a flock of other machines. It's not the downtown YMCA, but it does the job.

Recently, this family-owned operation became a 24-hour fitness center—meaning that they installed some electronic fob-activated locks and shortened their normal office hours. Now, for a $20 deposit, you can get a key fob, and even on the day after Thanksgiving, you are free to pump iron any time you want.

So there I was, one of only three people in the building, sweating away on the elliptical machine. Nearby, an older man was doing leg presses, and in the far quadrant of the room, another guy was fiddling around with those large disc-shaped metal things that I don't pay much attention to.

Just then a young man approached the front door of the gym from the outside. He had a beard and wore a hooded sweatshirt. He walked straight up to the door and went to open it in a way that showed he had been in the gym many times before. When it didn't give, he pulled harder.

He obviously didn't know about the fobs because then his eyes flicked confusedly to each of us inside the building. He pulled at the door again. He pulled again, shaking the handle. A moment later, the flat of his hand came up, hovered in the air for a second, and slammed on the frame of the glass window next to him.

We'd all been instructed, when the owner gave us our fobs, that we were under no circumstances allowed to let people in during closed hours. So we didn't move. But I wished that I wasn't situated so very close to the door—just a few yards from him.

His reaction to finding himself closed out, seeing us inside, and having none of us move to help him all occurred within just a few seconds. After shaking the door, he looked at each of us again, one at a time. Then his gaze was suddenly angry, and just as suddenly, he became embarrassed. In a swift movement, he turned his head to the ground, shrugged, and turned, walking away to the next store over as if he'd never intended to get inside at all.

I nearly jumped down and ran after the young man, just to explain to him about the fobs so he would know the new system. But then I remembered that the doors were locked from inside too, and the fob was in my locker. He was already disappearing down the sidewalk anyway.

Watching this young man's almost wild reaction to being locked out was interesting and strangely sad to me. Why did he react like that? Was it just because of his thwarted desire for exercise? Was it simply the frustration of coming all that way for nothing? Probably it was; anyone with a short temper might have reacted that way. But his eyes, which I was close enough to see, and his strange embarrassment and pretense at the end reminded me of something else.

It reminded me of a wild, panicky fear in my own heart: the fear of being left out.

For there to be a relationship, family, or a circle of friends that I want to participate in or that I once participated in and am now not allowed to be a part of—this is one of the deepest fears of my soul. Don't lock the door on me. Not when I can see you in there, enjoying yourselves. What is it that got you in there, anyway? Somebody forgot to tell me. They changed the locks and didn't give me the new key.

We are told by every wise voice around us that life isn't about what you have. It's about who you know. In all the glories that God has gifted upon man, the glory of loving relationship is the highest (1 Corinthians 13:13). This desire, like most of the good desires that our Maker placed in our hearts, becomes idolatrous only when it becomes a demand or when it tries to climb out of its natural boundaries.

Envy is among the ways that relational desire turns to sin.

Look around you. Are there good marriages that you resent, simply because they aren't yours? Are there circles of friends that you wish, in your private moments, to abolish, simply because there doesn't seem to be room for you in them? Are there people you feel bitterness toward because of the love they enjoy with their parents and siblings? Or maybe you just want to break into Pi Kappa Delta, and you burn because you've been overlooked. Maybe you can't understand why your friends Tom and Harry get along so very well together and why they don't seem to seek you out nearly as often as each other.

It might seem like all these things are mixed up with the influence and charm we talked about in an earlier chapter. After all, if charisma draws people in, then it must be that charismatic people have lots of good relationships.

But I haven't found this to be the case in real life. The people who seem to have the best and most steady relationships—with spouse, family, and friends—aren't always the charming ones, and they aren't always known by a great number of people. In my experience, many of these are not flashy people at all. They lead fairly small lives in fairly small circles, but the bonds in their relationships are strong. Sometimes, these relationships aren't even fruit they're reaping from good seed that they sowed themselves. Sometimes, instead, the healthy relationships simply dropped into their lives—it's just the family they were born into, for instance, or a spouse who inexplicably picked them.

In the meantime, some of the most charming and influential

people in the world still struggle with the practice of relational intimacy. It's possible to draw a crowd around yourself without knowing any of the individuals in that crowd very well.

There is nothing more painful or ubiquitous to the human experience than loneliness. And there is no envy stronger and more bitter than the envy of another person's secure relationship. The bitterness is often proportional to the power of the need. We need to be known and loved, and we need it desperately. Even a scriptural view of human needs—acknowledging first our need for God— recognizes that, as the old song has it, "You're nobody till somebody loves you." We were dead, and then…we experienced God's love (Ephesians 2:4-5).

But God's love does not, in this age, instantly change the situation we are in. We still experience the curse on our relationships, and our desire for true connection is at the heart of our most secret hopes and desires and aches. We are still outside of the full eternal fellowship of God that is our eventual inheritance. This is why we still often feel "outside" and why we long so to be let back in.

So when we see another person enjoying an (apparently) unbroken version of our hearts' deepest desire, it can be hard to bear. Fatherless? Think of the pain you feel when you see a father praise his son. Marriage not what you hoped? Think of the stab you experience when you watch your friend's husband smile at her from across the room. Friendless? Think of the hot-and-cold sensation you feel when you walk up to acquaintances of yours who are best friends—two friends you'd do almost anything to be on more intimate terms with.

There is glory in the adoration of the new lover, the blush of the beloved daughter, the hand-squeeze of the intimate friend. It is a glory almost too great to gaze upon unflinching.

Five Things We Know About Relationship from Scripture

There are five things that we can learn from the Bible about how the glories of relationship affect and are affected by our spiritual lives.

1. God's Glory Is a Relational Glory

We worship a triune God. He is a God whose existence has always centered on a triad of relational glory. The community of love that is sustained between the Father, Son, and Spirit is unparalleled, and it is from this Holy Family that all other families on earth are named (Ephesians 3:15).

Every love that has ever existed between human beings is a facsimile love derived from that triad relationship. Love was invented here.

The love in the Trinity is like a spring on a mountaintop that brings forth only an obscurely scented, sweet water. The water is carried down from the source and dispersed in precious drops around the world—sweetening dinner tables, churches, marriage beds, and playgrounds. Wherever you smell the inimitable scent of this water, you must be reminded of its source on the mountaintop. This water can come only from one place.

Jesus, in his time on earth away from the immediate presence of the Father, seemed to leap at any chance to talk about the Father and his shared relationship. He was as eager as an immigrant in a foreign country who has a sudden chance to talk about his homeland. One imagines the glowing tones, the irrepressible smile, or the quiet solemnity with which he spoke the sweet name of his Father.

"I and the Father are one," he said (John 10:30).

And what else did he give up that was greater, really? In all the pains and inconveniences that the Christ experienced as a human man in a dusty ancient country, what did he give up to come here that was greater than this immediate presence of the Father?

Still, they communed. And Christ spoke of the Father as a man speaks of hope:

> "In that day you will ask in my name, and I do not say to you that I will ask the Father on your behalf; for the Father himself loves you, because you have loved me and have believed that I came from God. I came from the Father and have come into the world, and now I am leaving the world and going to the Father" (John 16:26-28).

2. We May Be Called to Lose Some of Our Closest Relationships for the Sake of Christ

It's hard enough to be reviled by the world at large for the sake of the gospel. But there is a closer and more painful loss that Jesus warned us to be prepared for—the loss of father, mother, sister, brother, spouse, and friend. These are the very relationships that we are called on to cultivate and tend with the most care and love. Yet Jesus said that if we value these more than the way of the cross, then we aren't worthy to call him Brother:

> Everyone who acknowledges me before men, I also will acknowledge before my Father who is in heaven, but whoever denies me before men, I also will deny before my Father who is in heaven.
>
> Do not think that I have come to bring peace to the earth. I have not come to bring peace, but a sword. For I have come to set a man against his father, and a daughter against her mother, and a daughter-in-law against her mother-in-law. And a person's enemies will be those of his own household. Whoever loves father or mother more than me is not worthy of me, and whoever loves son or daughter more than me is not worthy of me (Matthew 10:32-37).

If you are a Christian, be prepared for loss. In Luke 14, Jesus talks about a foolish person who begins a project or starts a war without knowing how much it will cost him to finish it. His implication is that when we commit to seeking after the "pearl of great value" (Matthew 13:46), we must be prepared for loss of even the most close and precious people in our lives.

Jesus isn't asking that we endure this loss without promise of reward, however. Instead, he blatantly offers us prizes:

> Peter said, "See, we have left our homes and followed you." And he said to them, "Truly, I say to you, there is no one who has left house or wife or brothers or parents or children, for the sake of the kingdom of God, who will not receive many times more in this time, and in the age to come eternal life" (Luke 18:28-30).

3. God Has Prepared a New Family for Us (the Church)

We've just finished talking about the relational losses we should be prepared to sustain as we live the Christian life. But we can just as truly say that obedience will improve many of our relationships. If we walk in obedience, practicing love the way we've been taught, we may experience strength and health in many of the relationships that God gives.

And some of our relationships will only be ours because of the new life we are living. In the church, God has ordained a new family, which for many believers may be the only community they are members of until the new heaven and the new earth.

Imperfect and toddling, the church is nevertheless a glorious bride that Christ is preparing for himself (Ephesians 5:25-27). Within this structure, we have the opportunity for relationship that is lasting and that sanctifies. There is intimacy within this structure, there is annoyance, there is growth, and there is grace.

This passage in Romans gives us enough to keep us busy in both this life and the next:

> Let love be genuine. Abhor what is evil; hold fast to what is good. Love one another with brotherly affection. Outdo one another in showing honor. Do not be slothful in zeal, be fervent in spirit, serve the Lord. Rejoice in hope, be patient in tribulation, be constant in prayer. Contribute to the needs of the saints and seek to show hospitality.
>
> Bless those who persecute you; bless and do not curse them. Rejoice with those who rejoice, weep with those who weep. Live in harmony with one another. Do not be haughty, but associate with the lowly. Never be wise in your own sight. Repay no one evil for evil, but give thought to do what is honorable in the sight of all. If possible, so far as it depends on you, live peaceably with all (Romans 12:9-18).

From this passage we can draw the following directives, among others.

Be diligent in loving. "Do not be slothful in zeal," says the passage. It also tells us to "rejoice in hope, be patient in tribulation, be constant in prayer," and specifically to contribute to needs of the saints and show hospitality. This is the work of loving. It is opening cans of beans and chopping vegetables. It is time spent in the prayer closet. It is attending a funeral and a graduation. Loving can put miles on your car and wear out your arms.

Be sacrificial in loving. This passage calls us to dig beneath the kind of acts that come easy to us. The acts of love described here run the gamut, addressing the whole person: physical needs, social needs, and spiritual needs.

This means that at some point our weak spots are going to come out. Perhaps we find it easy to put someone up for the night, to wash sheets and put a breakfast on the table, but we can't be bothered to have a conversation with her about the funeral she's in town for. Perhaps we go around telling people that we are praying for them without spending the time to do so—or without being willing to do anything that will help them out of their difficulty when it lies in our power. To love sacrificially means to examine the parts of yourself that you are least willing to give and then to practice, practice, practice giving them.

Be bold in loving. The kind of love commanded here is not for the timid. Look at the response commanded for those who weep: Weep with them. The way to associate with people who may embarrass you: Mix with them. Consider people your brothers, even though some of them may intimidate you. Live peaceably with all, so far as it depends on you, even though this most certainly will involve coming through conflict rather than avoiding it. In fact, there's no way to avoid conflict when you also are commanded to love and bless your enemy—enemies can't be avoided and served at the same time.

Be meek in loving. "Outdo one another in showing honor," says the passage. This is the only kind of competition allowed you in the pursuit of heaven. Also, notice the commands to "never be wise in your own sight," and to "bless those who persecute you; bless and do not curse them."

There is no faking true meekness. The false version always comes out looking something like Uriah Heep in *David Copperfield*, looking daggers at everyone and repeating the refrain about how "very 'umble" he is. Meekness means thinking less of yourself by thinking of yourself less.

The directives in Scripture for loving well are an invaluable guide for those of us who struggle with building good relationships. And for those who envy the good relationships enjoyed by others, we have an obvious and clear opportunity to join those whom we envy. We may not be able to enter their relationship in the same way with the same person, but we are certainly given free rein to cultivate bonds of love with all the people around us.

No matter what disadvantages we have—of personality, background, or temperament—if we practice love in these ways, then we will find ourselves coming to the end of our lives with better relationships than we had at the beginning of our lives. And through it all we'll be better formed for heaven, where loneliness is done away with forever.

4. We Must Trust God's Providence in Relationships

Whatever circumstances we find ourselves in, we must trust God's providence that we have the right people in our lives at the right time. It's true that we'll find people tend to respond to love well aimed. But there will still be many disappointments and losses in love.

And we may still find that our pride is not ministered to in the way we would like. Sometimes our desire for relationship is really just a desire for honor—we want to be respected and we want to be connected with people who are respected. Whether or not we are especially lonely, it can be mortifying not to have a spouse you want to show off in company or not to be able to speak your father's name with unblinking pride.

But this is not to be, not for all of us. God has carefully ordained a situation for each of us, at each stage in our lives, to promote growth. Sometimes the growth is painful and awkward. Sometimes it doesn't allow us to preen before our fellow men. Sometimes, because of the realities of sin and death, it is downright excruciating.

But every person God has placed in our lives is there for a reason, and if he withholds another kind of person from our lives, then he has a reason for that too.

The way to rest in God's relational lot for you is to fill yourself with the promises he has made:

> We know that for those who love God all things work together for good, for those who are called according to his purpose…What then shall we say to these things? If God is for us, who can be against us? He who did not spare his own Son but gave him up for us all, how will he not also with him graciously give us all things? (Romans 8:28,31-32).

5. We Are Children of God and Siblings of Christ

There is one relationship that we are promised as our right and heritage: we are children of God and siblings of Christ. In Jesus's descriptions of the love within the Trinity that we talked about earlier, he did much more than gloat about his communion with the Father. He put out an invitation—to us.

He invited us inside—to be part of the inner ring to end all inner rings:

> I will ask the Father, and he will give you another Helper, to be with you forever, even the Spirit of truth, whom the world cannot receive, because it neither sees him nor knows him. You know him, for he dwells with you and will be in you.
>
> I will not leave you as orphans; I will come to you. Yet a little while and the world will see me no more, but you will see me. Because I live, you also will live. In that day you will know that I am in my Father, and you in me, and I in you. Whoever has my commandments and keeps them, he it is who loves me. And he who loves me will be loved by my Father, and I will love him and manifest myself to him (John 14:16-21).

Jesus is claiming that we will actually be *in* the Father, *in* Christ, with the Holy Spirit *in* us. Somehow, we will be sitting on the mountaintop, bathing in the scented water we only caught whiffs of until now. In the following chapter, Christ commands obedience and love, saying that it will be a sign of our abiding in him in the mysterious way he described before. He also reminds us again of the fact that we are now "inside." He has treated us as friends—because he has let us in on his plans. This is not the act of a boss, but of a colleague.

> As the Father has loved me, so have I loved you. Abide in my love. If you keep my commandments, you will abide in my love, just as I have kept my Father's commandments and abide in his love. These things I have spoken to you, that my joy may be in you, and that your joy may be full.
>
> This is my commandment, that you love one another as I have loved you. Greater love has no one than this, that someone lay down his life for his friends. You are my friends if you do what I command you. No longer do I call you servants, for the servant does not know what his master is doing; but I have called you friends, for all that I have heard from my Father I have made known to you (John 15:9-15).

In Christ, we are friends and children of the Most High God. "I am sure," said Paul, "that neither death nor life, nor angels nor rulers, nor things present nor things to come, nor powers, nor height nor depth, nor anything else in all creation, will be able to separate us from the love of God in Christ Jesus our Lord" (Romans 8:38-39).

This should give pause to our grasping for membership in Pi Kappa Delta.

Discussion Questions

- Describe a time when you experienced the feeling of wishing that you were connected with different people than those God placed in your life (especially permanent relationships—family of origin, spouse, children).

- Do you ever experience the fear of being left out or overlooked for relationship? How do you respond?

- Have you ever been in a position to open your arms, or open the circle, to someone on the outside and neglected to do so? Are you currently in this position with someone whom you are holding at arm's length?

- The kind of love commanded in Romans 12 is diligent, sacrificial, bold, and meek. Which of these modes of love have been most difficult for you personally to practice?

10

Put Off, Put On

Jonathan made a covenant with David, because he loved him as his own soul. And Jonathan stripped himself of the robe that was on him and gave it to David, and his armor, and even his sword and his bow and his belt. And David went out and was successful wherever Saul sent him, so that Saul set him over the men of war. And this was good in the sight of all the people and also in the sight of Saul's servants.

1 SAMUEL 18:3-5

You don't want to be this way anymore. I know you don't.

Envy is the only sin I can think of that is really no fun at all. It begins in negative feelings of inferiority, progresses into nasty feelings of resentment, and then stagnates in a stewing, frothy mess of petty or belligerent offspring sins. Even when envy gets what it wants—the destruction or removal of another person's borrowed glory—it is left with empty energy that must be redirected to a new object of hatred.

None of this lights up any pleasure centers in anybody's brain. Gluttony, greed, lust, vanity, murder, pride, and all their cousins at least have that much going for them.

Thankfully for the Christian, it is both our right and our business to "put off your old self" and to "put on the new self" (Ephesians 4:22-24). I say "thankfully" because this is truly a mercy. The work of fighting sin is hard work, but it is merciful work too. To gain any kind of freedom from sin is a luxury that the world simply doesn't have.

And slavery to sin is a merciless slavery. Envy is a perfect example of that—a sin that requires all your heart, soul, mind, and strength and delivers you nothing (not even a lighted pleasure center) in return.

The Christian who battles the sin of envy may mistakenly feel that he is in more of a skirmish than a battle. Why? Because envy is so easy to keep a secret, even from oneself. And like other sins of the heart, the human imagination is always trying to relegate it to second place in the sin scale. *Envy can't be as dangerous as fornication because nobody ever sees it and it doesn't really hurt anyone.* Then, if envy ever produces natural offspring—other, more overt sins—our tendency is to cut off the sin that has flowered up out of it without attempting any harm to the envious root.

This attitude is terribly insufficient. Here are two good reasons to take envy seriously enough to pull out the big guns against it:

One, Scripture makes it clear that although man cares mostly for the outward appearance, God is concerned with the heart (1 Samuel 16:7). This means that all this business about envy being a "secret sin" is nonsense. God can see your envy and your fornication side by side as if they were two slugs lying next to each other in the sun. There are no secret sins.

Two, Scripture makes it clear that what is in the heart doesn't stay in the heart because, as Jesus observed on more than one occasion, it is out of the heart that the mouth speaks (Matthew 12:34; 15:18). Envy leads to action—like every other sin of the heart. Envy is not safe, it doesn't stay put, and it comes accompanied with the most open and shameful sister sins that you ever feared to fall into.

Four Virtues to Put On When You Put Off Envy

Envy is a monster, and you're going to have to do explosive, violent war with it. One of the ways Scripture models the fight with sin is through the "put off, put on" model outlined in Paul's letter to the Ephesians:

> That is not the way you learned Christ!—assuming that you have heard about him and were taught in him, as the truth is in Jesus, to put off your old self, which belongs to your former manner of life and is corrupt through deceitful desires, and to be renewed in the spirit of your minds, and to put on the new self, created after the likeness of God in true righteousness and holiness (Ephesians 4:20-24).

In the spirit of Ephesians 4, here are four virtues that you'll need to put on as you put off the sin of envy.

1. Put Off Envy by Putting On Love

The story of David and Jonathan is one that always takes my breath away. Jonathan is an example that I look to in wonder—who could have had a clearer temptation to envy than he had? Jonathan is the heir apparent when he meets David, who is set up by God to take over the monarchy (eventually). The writing is already on the wall, and instead of balking, Jonathan embraces his replacement.

Can you imagine yourself in this situation? I am moved to love Jonathan as I read; nobody could have handled this situation with more grace and cheerful sacrifice. How did he do it?

Apparently, he was motivated by love. He loved David as soon as he met him: loved him, 1 Samuel 18 repeatedly says, "as his own soul." So he literally strips himself of glory—takes his own robe and armor off—and gives it freely to David. Then, whenever he has the opportunity to act as David's enemy and shore up his own right to the throne, he instead acts as David's protector and advocate.

Jonathan shows us that love is the surest and most beautiful antidote to envy.

Love and envy are diametrically opposed. Scripture is explicit about this in one of the most famous definitions of love ever written, 1 Corinthians 13:

> Love is patient and kind; *love does not envy* or boast; it is not arrogant or rude. It does not insist on its own way; it is not irritable or resentful; it does not rejoice at wrongdoing, but rejoices with the truth. Love bears all things, believes all things, hopes all things, endures all things. Love never ends (1 Corinthians 13:4-8, emphasis added).

The full passage here on love declares it the most important virtue there is. Even faith and hope will pass away, it says, but love is for both this world and the world to come.

In fact, by the time this passage was written, Jesus had already established the idea of love as the most important thing. When asked to condense the whole law into one statement, Jesus condensed it to two: "You shall love the Lord your God with all your heart and with all your soul and with all your mind" and "You shall love your neighbor as yourself" (Matthew 22:37-39).

If love and envy cannot coexist because love doesn't envy, then love will surely be a great aid to us in banishing envy from our hearts and lives.

The practical tips here for acting out the motions of love are just that—motions. Yes, I'm recommending that you "fake it until you make it," in the case of love. The tips in this chapter major on behavior over emotion, because although emotion is difficult to generate out of thin air, it does tend to follow action around on a leash.

Show love by thanking God for the success of the person you envy. Jesus commanded us to pray for our enemies as one way of doing good to them (Matthew 5:43-48). This is a great way to start showing love toward the person you envy.

Now to be clear—is she actually your enemy? Maybe. Maybe not. It's possible that she has actually set herself up against you, seeing you as the rival that you are and directing hatred right back at you. But it's also possible—and maybe more likely—that she's just a friend or acquaintance of yours who has no idea you feel this enmity toward her, or at least she hasn't identified the weird vibes she's getting from you as envious hatred.

Either way, the envious heart turns even friends into enemies. Whether or not it's accurate, your heart believes that this person is an enemy to your happiness. That means that you can pray for your friend (whom you are thinking of as an enemy) and still be obedient to Jesus's word here.

When you pray, thank God for her and for her borrowed glory. Thank him for granting her success.

Show love by asking God for the further success of the person you envy. That's right. Pray specifically for her continued success, especially in whichever borrowed glory it is you are envying her for.

This means that if you have a friend who is getting all As and just got a free ride to Yale, then your order of business is to pray that she would keep getting As at Yale. If your beautiful cousin just started dating a guy who is everything you ever dreamed of, then pray that they would honor God in their relationship and begin to grow strong together in their love, as the Lord wills.

Ask for things for your friends the way you would ask for things for yourself. Yes, this means giving thought to their whole person and spiritual state and attempting to ask wisely for things that would do them long-term good, but also it means not limiting your prayers to things like, "Lord, I pray that you would protect Rachel from becoming prideful."

Show love by enjoying the borrowed glory of the person you envy. Most of the glories we've discussed in this book are not possessions but personal traits, such as beauty, talent, charm, and more. The wonderful thing about these gifts from the Father is that they can be possessed by one person and enjoyed by others simultaneously.

With the borrowed human glories that involve some kind of personal trait, God has ordained that one person's gifting provides another person's enjoyment. When you are spending time with your friend, her charm and humor is something you can belly laugh over. When you are listening to your coworker give a talk at a professional convention, you've got a chance both to learn something and to worship the Father for making her so good at what she does. The fact that your sister plays really good music means—to state the obvious—that you have the opportunity to *hear* really good music.

Go through the exercise of doing what you may have avoided for a long time—gaze upon the glory with an unflinching gaze. Look for opportunities to praise the Father for what he has made.

Show love by praising the person you envy. Under normal circumstances, praising something is both a natural result of enjoying it and part of the process of enjoying it. This means that for you to silently, stoically sit and soak in the borrowed glory of a friend or acquaintance without expressing admiration would be unnatural. It would truncate the exercise of enjoyment. It would also waste a wonderful opportunity for you to do battle with envy.

Ephesians 4:29 commands, "Let no corrupting talk come out of your mouths, but only such as is good for building up, as fits the occasion, that it may give grace to those who hear." What talk is more corrupting than the natural talk of an envious person in polite society? They find ways of inserting a barb into every compliment. They find ways of gossiping without openly declaring anything.

The alternative, according to this passage, should fill us with joy and possibility. We could instead use words that are "good for building up," that "fit the occasion," that "give grace." Is that possible? Could we do that?

Not only can we—we must. And we may find that it is very difficult to praise a person warmly with our mouths and continue to hate them with our hearts. So become a "fan" of the person you envy. Praise openly where praise is due. Don't flatter, and don't praise in such a way that you are taking a borrowed glory and treating it as ultimate. There is a way to tell a pretty girl that she is pretty without implying that to be pretty is the most important thing in her life or yours. There is a way to graciously praise a person's book without openly worshipping him.

This is part of the reason that I dragged you through all those topical chapters on the specific borrowed glories. I meant to give you a real sense of what it's like to experience each specific borrowed glory secondhand, but I also meant to use Scripture to place each of these borrowed glories into an appropriate place of significant insignificance. The goal is neither to ignore the borrowed glories nor to grovel before them.

To acknowledge God as the source and author of it all and to see the glory as creaturely and derivative is the only way this can be done. This frees us up to praise our neighbor naturally and freely.

2. Put Off Envy by Putting On Diligence

Envy and diligence have a hard time coexisting. Envy, you remember, is more destructive than it is productive. This means that when envy sees another person doing well, it is usually more concerned with pulling the other person down than clambering up to stand next to them.

Remember the Bible's description of Cain and his fury over Abel's accepted sacrifice? When God rebuked Cain, he gave him the simple advice that our mothers have probably given many of us: "Why are you angry, and why has your face fallen? If you do well, will you not be accepted? And if you do not do well, sin is crouching at the door. Its desire is for you, but you must rule over it" (Genesis 4:6-7).

That is part of the rankling nature of envy. For many of us, part of the burn is that we know what the other person has is not really unattainable for us. They are well liked because they are kind to other people—we could do that. They are succeeding at work because they put in 100 percent effort—we could if we wanted to. Their home is neat and clean because they make it a priority to keep it that way—it could be our priority too.

Now as we also saw in many of our topical chapters, some of the glories are completely out of our hands. We can't generate artistic talent out of thin air. We can't become football stars by training hard if we're five feet tall and 100 pounds. Part of wisdom is understanding our limitations and recognizing areas of our lives where God simply hasn't gifted us.

But in a real sense, even if you can never attain another person's level of ability, knowing that you put your absolute best work in is a balm for envy that there are no substitutes for. Proverbs gives us all the evidence we need that this is true:

Do you see a man skillful in his work?
>   He will stand before kings,
>   He will not stand before obscure men
>   (Proverbs 22:29).

This proverb communicates the serene confidence of the hard worker. He stands before kings without shame. Surely this means he can stand before a person of superior glory, knowing that his work represents his best and that this is enough.

If you say, "Behold, we did not know this,"
>   does not he who weighs the heart perceive it?
>   Does not he who keeps watch over your soul know it,
>   and will he not repay man according to his work?
>   (Proverbs 24:12).

This proverb shoots down the excuse-making that envy often resorts to. "Well, if I'd have known that the boss was going to do performance reviews this week, then I would have been more serious about what I was doing, and Smith wouldn't have been the man of the hour…" This proverb is a silencer: *You didn't know? Doesn't really matter, does it?*

The practice and cultivation of diligence is an irreplaceable weapon in the fight against envy (and against many other sins). Not only that, but it is a way of serving your Lord Jesus Christ. A verse we looked at a couple of chapters ago is worth repeating. "Whatever you do, work heartily, as for the Lord and not for men," Paul urged the Colossians, "knowing that from the Lord you will receive the inheritance as your reward" (3:23-24).

Throw your whole mind and soul into loving God through your work: vocational work, housework, relational work, creative work, hospitality, physical exercise, spiritual exercise, and ministry.

Keeping your hands busy with honest labor is a great way to drown out the idle, wasteful sin of envy. And as you do this work, you should do it with your proper reward in mind: an inheritance that involves hearing, "Well done, good and faithful servant."

There is such a thing as healthy competition, and if used rightly, it can stir us up to love and good works (Hebrews 10:24). As we have seen, in Romans 12:10, Paul encouraged the Romans to love one another with brotherly affection and to "outdo one another in showing honor." This is clearly a form of competition, but it is a healthy one. It's a race to see who can love the other best.

3. Put Off Envy by Putting On Humility

It's no surprise that pride is in the laundry list of sister sins that envy appears with (Mark 7:22). Just as Scripture makes it clear that love and envy are diametrically opposed, Scripture also makes it clear that humility and envy are diametrically opposed. "Do nothing from selfish ambition or conceit," Paul wrote to the Philippians, "but in humility count others more significant than yourselves" (2:3).

The opposite of envy? Love. Another opposite of envy? Humility. We've talked at length about hatred as an ingredient in envy, but we've not been as explicit about another ingredient: thwarted pride.

Envy doesn't feel like a sin of pride because it is so often the affliction of the underdog. The envious man at first glance has an inferiority complex, not a superiority complex. He sees the person he envies as having an advantage over him; this is one of the reasons that envy is so difficult to confess. For a heart already smarting under the feeling of inferiority, to confess "I've been feeling that you are better than me, and I've been hating you for it," is tantamount to deliberately burning oneself in the most tender of places.

But envy is not actually a humble sin. It is a sin of pride—pride that has been thwarted. The envious woman believes that all glory and honor should go to herself. She can't stand to witness the glory of another human being because she wants it all. When she doesn't get it, her thwarted pride gives birth to envy.

If we want to take seriously the words of Paul in Philippians, that means considering others as more significant than ourselves. This feels like an impossible task until we remember that God has already promised to give us success through the work of Christ. Let's read the rest of the passage cited above in Philippians 2:

> Do nothing from selfish ambition or conceit, but in humility count others more significant than yourselves. Let each of you look not only to his own interests, but also to the interests of others. Have this mind among yourselves, *which is yours in Christ Jesus*, who, though he was in the form of God, did not count equality with God a thing to be grasped, but emptied himself, by taking the form of a servant, being born in the likeness of men. And being found in human form, he humbled himself by becoming obedient to the point of death, even death on a cross (Philippians 2:3-8).

This is incredible. We're in the middle of a discussion about humility as an antidote to envy. We read in this passage that we're to "do nothing from selfish ambition" but instead to "count others more significant than yourselves."

But how? we ask. Obviously being unselfish is good—everybody agrees on that—but how do we manage it? Considering others as more important than ourselves goes against every grain in us.

If we keep reading, then the passage answers all these doubts. This mind *can* be found among brothers and sisters in Christ, as it is actually ours already "in Christ Jesus." We're being transformed into the image of our Lord, and our Lord—despite the glory he came from—was the picture of humility. He didn't grasp at equality with God, his only peer. Instead, he emptied himself, taking the form of a servant, becoming a man. Then he humbled himself further by giving himself up to humiliation and death.

So how can we do this simple but seemingly impossible thing of putting off prideful envy and putting on humility? We must look to Christ. He is our own king, and he is a king who humbled himself unto death. Like Aslan in C.S. Lewis's *The Lion, the Witch, and the Wardrobe,* he was a lion who lay down and let a witch cut him open. He was, in fact, a lamb. What can we say in the face of such humility except "Lord, [wash] not my feet only, but also my hands and my head!" (John 13:9).

And in the end, what happened to Christ and what is promised to us—glory following humility—is a principle echoed in Proverbs 29:23: "One's pride will bring him low, but he who is lowly in spirit will obtain honor."

4. Put Off Envy by Putting On Transparency

Confession of sin, while fun for no one, is vital to the Christian life and the eventual defeat of that sin. Confession of sin falls into two major categories: confession to God and confession to man.

Be transparent by confessing the sin of envy to God. You may remember 1 John 1:8-10: "If we say we have no sin, we deceive ourselves, and the truth is not in us. If we confess our sins, he is faithful and just to forgive us our sins and to cleanse us from all unrighteousness. If we say we have not sinned, we make him a liar, and his word is not in us."

Envy is insidious and doesn't like to be named. To confess it to God and ask for forgiveness will mean first that we have to know it for what it is.

Remember the way David described his own experience of concealing and confessing:

> When I kept silent, my bones wasted away
>   through my groaning all day long.
> For day and night your hand was heavy upon me;
>   my strength was dried up as by the heat of summer. Selah
>
> I acknowledged my sin to you,
>   and I did not cover my iniquity;
> I said, "I will confess my transgressions to the Lord,"
>   and you forgave the iniquity of my sin
>   (Psalm 32:3-5).

Notice something about this passage: The relief that David found wasn't in confession to the public or to his peers in a 12-step meeting. His first and primary business was to confess to God. This is what brought relief to his bones, to his dried-up strength. He found true and complete forgiveness of sin from God before going to others to confess it.

Confession directly to God has many purposes, but here are two of the most important: First, confessing sin is necessary for true repentance, which is a vital part of both our justification and our ongoing sanctification. Second, confessing sin means putting glasses on our deceitful heart so that it can't help but see our sin more clearly.

As we just read, 1 John promises that if we confess our sins, Jesus is faithful and just to forgive us our sins and to cleanse us from all unrighteousness. This removes all the fear of acknowledging our sin. How could we be afraid? There are such rewards waiting for us if we are obedient to this passage!

This means that as you walk up the aisle at church, recognize

a familiar object of your envy, and feel a stab of displeasure to see
him smiling happily at his wife, you can name that sin for what it
is immediately and confess it to God. This means that if you have
struggled for 20 years to be civil to your sister because she was the
family favorite, then you can begin immediately to confess your sin
to God as often as it crops up, calling it by name. This means that if
you are doing well but have occasional moments of anger when you
hear of somebody getting a promotion or taking a trip, then you can
confess the sin of envy immediately to God.

Over time, you will be less and less deceived about the nature of
your reactions to these things. You will be more and more willing
to battle against the sin in the other ways mentioned in this chapter.
You will find yourself more dependent on the throne of grace, and
freer to acknowledge your sin to others.

Which brings us to our next point:

*Be transparent by confessing the sin of envy to Christian brothers
and sisters.* James 5:16 commands us to do something terrifying
and unnatural: "Confess your sins to one another and pray for one
another, that you may be healed. The prayer of a righteous person
has great power as it is working."

Well, that's a tall order.

Imagine having to sit down with the object of your envy and lay
your cards on the table. "I need to confess something to you. I've
been resenting your success. I've been envious, and it's made me pull
away from you and occasionally gossip about you. I understand if
this is hard to hear, but I'm working hard to fight the sin of envy in
my life, and I need your prayers and your compassion."

This is a hard pill to even think about swallowing. You'd be
admitting your weakness to them. You'd be admitting that you
think they're better than you are in this particular area. You'd be
asking for their help because without their mercy it will be very

difficult to keep up the struggle against envy. And then—I've said it before and I'll say it again—there's the uniquely shameful nature of the sin. By confessing, you'd be admitting to one of the dirtiest, most low-down, repulsive sins in the book, one that people around you simply never seem to mention.

But confession may be necessary if you want to do earnest battle with it.

There are a few things to consider before you go rushing pell-mell into an emotional sit-down with your sister-in-law. The scriptural command to confess sin to fellow Christians is more complex than the command to confess your sins to God. Confession to God should be immediate and continual and comprehensive. But when it comes to confessing to others, tact and prudence must come into play.

Like another dangerous thought-life sin—lust—mentioning the sin of envy to the individual you are sinning against can cause more problems than it solves *in some cases*. So here are some general principles that may help you sort through the sticky question of confessing envy to another person.

Let the confession be as wide or as narrow as the sin itself. This means that you need to think honestly about the extent and consequences of the envy. Has it gone on for 20 years and ruined your relationship with your sister? Has it led you to other visible sin like creating a rumor, destroying property, insulting a person to her face, or physically harming someone? Or was it only a momentary thought against a colleague that you were able to squelch before it flowered? This should help guide you in deciding whether confession to the individual would be helpful or harmful.

Determine whether the envy is momentary or long-term. I personally have experienced two kinds of envy: one is a kind that attaches itself to a specific person and oppresses the relationship for years at a time, becoming obsessive and mystifying the other person. The other is a flash-in-the-pan envy. It is not concerned with a specific person but flares up momentarily in response to meeting someone for the first time or hearing about something good that has happened to an acquaintance or friend. The latter kind is often put down pretty quickly and doesn't give ongoing trouble.

I am much less likely to recommend confession of the flash-in-the-pan envy. Not because it isn't sinful and destructive, but because if we were to go around telling everybody every thought we had about them, it would create an atmosphere of suspicion and callousness. Like the momentary struggles with lust that we experience, it would be counterproductive to instantly bring our thoughts to our mouths every time they became sinful.

But in the case of those lasting and mighty battles with envy—often against those closest to you—confession may be necessary to restoring the relationship.

Identify whether the relationship has been damaged by your envy. The need to confess depends on whether the relationship has been damaged by the envy. If it is an acquaintance from work and you know he has no idea that you're feeling envious, then it could be damaging to have your first move of intimacy be a confession of hate-filled envy. If it is your best friend and you've cooled toward her because of your envy—and she knows it—then there is no way to make amends without confessing what's going on behind it all. In one case, confession could be damaging; and in another case, it could be healing.

Ask yourself this, honestly: Would confession build a further rift between you or help heal the relationship? Be willing to go through the discomfort to get to the restored friendship on the other side. Don't fool yourself into thinking you're keeping the peace when really what you're doing is settling for a loss of intimacy.

This is not a fun battle. It's not the kind that you can get on Instagram and humble-brag about, as if you were running a 5K to support the local animal shelter. It's private, uncomfortable, unflattering, and hard work. It's going to require a relentless honesty; only the keen edge of God's Word will be sharp enough to separate the thoughts and intentions of your heart (Hebrews 4:12). But the incredible mercy of our heavenly Father is such that he exposes us only to heal us. Where Satan is happy to lay open our innards to jeer and mock at their ugliness, only the God-man who laid himself down is willing to open us up, do the necessary surgery without flinching or mocking, and close up the incision as if it never was.

Be willing to do battle. Your joy in the Lord, your testimony of his goodness, and your relationships with his image bearers are all at stake.

Discussion Questions

- "Put on love by praising the person you envy." Have you ever been on the receiving end of well-placed praise that was edifying to you? Describe the experience.

- "Put off envy by putting on humility." Envy doesn't seem like a sin of pride because it is the affliction of the underdog. How are envy and pride actually related?

- "Put off envy by putting on transparency." Confessing envy to God is a nonnegotiable, but what are some situations when it may not be helpful to confess envy to the object of your envy?

- What are some excuses you might be using to get yourself off the hook of the very uncomfortable process of confessing envy?

11

The Eyes That Matter: Why We Need God's Approval After All

To please God...to be a real ingredient in the divine happiness...to be loved by God, not merely pitied, but delighted in as an artist delights in his work or a father in a son—it seems impossible, a weight or burden of glory which our thoughts can hardly sustain. But so it is.

C.S. LEWIS, *The Weight of Glory*

My husband, Justin, told me once that when he daydreamed as a boy, the daydream was usually about saving people. He imagined a fire or a burglar coming to his school or his home, and he imagined saving the day, his mom, and maybe Sissy Hendricks, who sat two rows behind him at Defeated Elementary School.[1]

These daydreams were always crowned with praise and admiration. First, his crush would be shyly appreciative of the heroism that had saved her life from danger. Then, either his dad or his teacher would say something like, "Well done, son. Don't know what would have happened if you weren't here. Nobody but you could have pulled 12 children out of a burning building, including Sissy Hendricks."

Would it have made any sense to young Justin if we'd told him at this age, "Hey, I don't know why your daydreams always end with recognition from these specific important people in your life. It would be better if you were recognized by this committee—it's very official. It's called the Heroism Recognition Committee, and it's full of people you don't know who are experts in heroism"?

This would have been nonsense to little Justin. Because when you're a nine-year-old boy and sitting two rows in front of Sissy Hendricks, all you really care about is (1) *What does Dad think about me?* (2) *What do Mom and the teachers think about me?* and (3) *What does Sissy Hendricks think about me?*

It would also be nonsense to Justin if you told him that he shouldn't be daydreaming about saving people from danger. "Everybody wants to be the hero, Justin. How about this? What if you were the world's best bed maker? Now that would be something. Just sit there a while and imagine the glory of being the world's best bed maker."

Even young Justin would know that when people need to be saved from danger, the need is much direr than the need for someone to get the covers into a perfect tuck. The need is greater, so the glory is greater. The job can only be done by a hero, so the job comes with a hero's honor.

Justin knew, even as a child, that it matters who you get recognition from. He also knew that it matters what you get recognition for.

As adults, we have a wider jury of peers. We now have parents, spouses, children, teachers, bosses, friends, and the whole internet to impress, although there are a few specific people we especially want to hear praise from. But despite the apparent sophistication of our accomplishments and our network of witnesses, many of us still live in the daydreamer's desk at Defeated Elementary School. We desire, above all else, to get some final stamp of approval that will not wash off.

The Eyes That Matter

C.S. Lewis often wrote about this feeling of unmet hunger. He imagined scene after scene, in book after book, of the final moment when we finally meet the object of our hunger. In the Chronicles of Narnia, in his essays, in his space trilogy, in the novel *Till We Have Faces*, and even in *The Screwtape Letters*, Lewis has his readers finally meet the Lord (or a near representation of the Lord) and experience a consummation of shock, awe, joy, pain, transformation, and approval. In the end, his characters always find that there is a Person at the other end of their desires. The Person is named as Aslan, or the West-wind, or the God of the Bible.

But his descriptions of these encounters blow us away every time and move us to tears again and again as they tug at the desire of our hearts. Here is one conversation from *Till We Have Faces*, between two sisters, one of whom has seen a god:

> "And then—at last—for a moment—I saw him."
>
> "Saw whom?"
>
> "The west-wind."
>
> "*Saw* it?"
>
> "Not it; him. The god of the wind; West-wind himself."
>
> "Were you awake, Psyche?"
>
> "Oh, it was no dream. One can't dream things like that, because one's never seen things like that. He was in human shape. But you couldn't mistake him for a man. Oh, Sister, you'd understand if you'd seen. How can I make you understand? You've seen lepers?"
>
> "Well, of course."
>
> "And you know how healthy people look beside a leper?"

"You mean—healthier, ruddier than ever?"

"Yes. Now we, beside the gods, are like lepers beside us…When I saw West-wind I was neither glad nor afraid (at first). I felt ashamed."

"But what of? Psyche, they hadn't stripped you naked or anything?"

"No, no, Maia. Ashamed of looking like a mortal— ashamed of being a mortal."

"But how could you help that?"

"Don't you think the things people are most ashamed of are the things they can't help?"[2]

Later on in *Till We Have Faces*, the second character in that interchange describes her own first encounter with a god:

In the centre of the light was something like a man. It is strange that I cannot tell you its size. Its face was far above me, yet memory does not show the shape as a giant's. And I do not know whether it stood, or seemed to stand, on the far side of the water or on the water itself.

Though this light stood motionless, my glimpse of the face was as swift as a true flash of lightning. I could not bear it for longer. Not my eyes only, but my heart and blood and very brain were too weak for that. A monster…would have subdued me less than the beauty this face wore. And I think anger (what men call anger) would have been more supportable than the passionless and measureless rejection with which it looked upon me. Though my body crouched where I could almost have touched his feet, his eyes seemed to send me from him to an endless distance. He rejected, denied, answered, and (worst of all), he knew, all I had thought, done or been.[3]

Lewis often made reference to the shame of being a human and sinful. He described it as the feeling of being naked and unworthy to meet with God or one of his messengers.

This shame is at the heart of every pain that we live with as fallen humans. Lewis rightly believed that removal of this shame, and the replacement of this shame with recognition from the Eyes That Matter, is at the heart of our most secret and glorious hopes. A boy is concerned with the eyes of his father, mother, and the Sissy Hendrickses of his life. As an adult, the eyes that concern him may change, and his ideas of heroism may change. But throughout it all, there is a constant. The Eyes That Matter are always there, and those other judges of his worth as a person are only stand-ins for this final voice. To be declared good, worthy, and honorable by these eyes is the only stamp that has ever truly mattered. This has always been a desire too great to be hoped for, too deep in his blood to be spoken of aloud.

And here we come to one of my favorite essays of all time, *The Weight of Glory*. This essay was instrumental in getting me thinking about the themes of this book, and if I could have just printed it in full as a chapter of this book, I would have. Since I can't, you need to go find it and read it.

> I can imagine someone saying that he dislikes my idea of heaven as a place where we are patted on the back. But proud misunderstanding is behind that dislike. In the end that Face which is the delight or terror of the universe must be turned upon each of us either with one expression or with the other, either conferring glory inexpressible or inflicting shame that can never be cured or disguised. I read in a periodical the other day that the fundamental thing is how we think of God. By God Himself, it is not! How God thinks of us is not only

more important, but infinitely more important. Indeed, how we think of Him is of no importance except insofar as it is related to how He thinks of us. It is written that we shall "stand before" Him, shall appear, shall be inspected. The promise of glory is the promise, almost incredible and only possible by the work of Christ, that some of us, that any of us who really chooses, shall actually survive that examination, shall find approval, shall please God. To please God…to be a real ingredient in the divine happiness…to be loved by God, not merely pitied, but delighted in as an artist delights in his work or a father in a son—it seems impossible, a weight or burden of glory which our thoughts can hardly sustain. But so it is.[4]

The Eyes That Matter in Scripture

For the Christian, this consummation of desire is not just a hope but a promise we have from those very Eyes That Matter. First Corinthians 8:3 promises that "if anyone loves God, he is known by God."

To be known by God—what an answer to the deepest desire of our hearts! Not only to know God, but to be known by him. To have the Eyes That Matter look on us finally with recognition and approval rather than dismissal and anger—because we wear the garments his Son purchased for us.

Here's the part that is difficult to believe, too wonderful to bear, and only possible because of the garments that the Son purchased. There's a guarantee. It is promised to the ones who hunger for the glory that only the Eyes That Matter can confer:

1. *Intimacy and approval.* We'll be known, yes, *known*, by "he who searches hearts," according to Romans 8:27. We have already been looked on by the Judge and pronounced righteous with the Son's righteousness.

2. *Transformation.* But there's more. Somehow Christ has worked it so that those who love God will be really conformed into Christ's own image.

This is why the guarantee—it's all being done by his own hands. We are predestined, called, justified, and then…glorified. Read it for yourself:

> He who searches hearts knows what is the mind of the Spirit, because the Spirit intercedes for the saints according to the will of God. And we know that for those who love God all things work together for good, for those who are called according to his purpose. For those whom he foreknew he also predestined to be conformed to the image of his Son, in order that he might be the firstborn among many brothers. And those whom he predestined he also called, and those whom he called he also justified, and those whom he justified he also glorified (Romans 8:27-31).

See how there are two necessary elements to the good news contained in this passage. If either of them was missing, the passage would no longer contain good news.

God's full and complete knowledge of us. "He who searches hearts" is the One who calls us. And "those whom he foreknew" are the people he has predestined and called and justified and glorified. If God didn't know us fully, there would be only a half joy in our glorification, like getting married to someone who adores you but doesn't know about your love child. God, the Eyes That Matter, must look upon us and know us fully in order for heaven to promise any joy. What kind of joy would it be if we were justified and glorified and then impersonally cranked along a conveyor belt to be processed into heaven's bliss? We need nothing less than to know and be known by our Maker.

God's transformation of us. "All things work together for good, for those who are called according to [God's] purpose," but how could that be true if we weren't going to be "conformed to the image of his Son"? We are accepted and justified on the basis of what that Son has already done for us. But wouldn't our joy be incomplete if we were then left to an eternity of inglorious struggle with sin and frailty? Instead, the chain of promise in Romans 8 goes beyond justification. Because "those whom he justified he also glorified." Those whom he predestined were predestined to be conformed to the image of his Son.

We don't want God to simply look upon us, withhold condemnation and judgment, and move on. Neither do we want him to simply say, "Despite everything, and because of what my Son has done, you can remain with me as you are. I'll choose not to see your ugly parts." We want to be transformed—to take beauty and worth into ourselves, to have the sin banished from our hearts completely, and to be someone who can stand before the King unashamed and glory in him. We want, in short, what was described in the Lewis passage above: to be "loved by God, not merely pitied, but delighted in as an artist delights in his work or a father in a son."

Conversely, the greatest warning in Scripture for the end of time is that you may find yourself formally *unknown*—for eternity. Jesus described the scene in Matthew. He said that in the final day many people will call on his name and point out the many spiritual things they've done for him—casting out demons, prophesying, the works. "And then," Jesus said, "will I declare to them, 'I never knew you; depart from me, you workers of lawlessness'" (Matthew 7:23).

This is worse than that dream when you walk up to your brother or best friend or spouse and tap them on the shoulder, and they turn and look at you with the eyes of a stranger. It's worse than the moment a child runs up and grabs a woman's knees and then finds she's not her mother.

This is a strangerhood that is complete—and final. It is a refusal of recognition from the one being in all the universe whom it is most important for you to be recognized by. It is light turning away from you, because you have refused to acknowledge the difference between light and darkness.

Notice that in Jesus's description of Judgment Day, the judge's sentence isn't phrased the way you might have expected. Rather than talking about hellfire or some of the other imagery we find elsewhere in Scripture, Jesus will utter a verdict in two terrible sentences: "I never knew you; depart from me." And this is enough; it is a death toll on joy and the beginning of suffering—forever.

The Lamb Who Was Slain

I remember a specific watershed day in my Christian walk when I was still a fairly new believer. I had been through a very difficult month or two, struggling and losing in a battle with besetting sin.

I was discouraged and disgruntled. My heart was heavy with the fear that perhaps my conversion had not been true—or that perhaps my faith and hope in the God of Scripture had been misplaced. I was tired of the world, tired of watching the foibles of other people, and tired of witnessing the wickedness of my own heart.

One night I found myself attending a Christian conference because it was being held at my church. One of the speakers read from Revelation.

> Then I saw in the right hand of him who was seated on the throne a scroll written within and on the back, sealed with seven seals. And I saw a mighty angel proclaiming with a loud voice, "Who is worthy to open the scroll

and break its seals?" And no one in heaven or on earth
or under the earth was able to open the scroll or to look
into it, and I began to weep loudly because no one was
found worthy to open the scroll or to look into it (Revelation 5:1-4).

By this point in the chapter, I was weeping myself. I identified
with the weeping of John, and I had never identified with it before.

No one is worthy. In the absence of worth, there is nothing but
hunger and desolation. Looking at my own actions and the actions
of those around me, there was no one worthy, not really. If there is
nothing good, nothing worthy, nothing glorious, then where can
these things come from? What is there to do but weep?

There is no one to open the scroll.

Then the preacher read on:

> One of the elders said to me, "Weep no more; behold, the
> Lion of the tribe of Judah, the Root of David, has con-
> quered, so that he can open the scroll and its seven seals."

> And between the throne and the four living creatures
> and among the elders I saw a Lamb standing, as though
> it had been slain...

> Then I looked, and I heard around the throne and the
> living creatures and the elders the voice of many angels,
> numbering myriads of myriads and thousands of thou-
> sands, saying with a loud voice,

> "Worthy is the Lamb who was slain,
>   to receive power and wealth and wisdom
>   and might and honor and glory and blessing!"
>   (Revelation 5:5-6,11-12).

And even now, as I reread this passage, I weep. Such joy fills my
heart as I follow John's emotion from despair to hope to exultation

when the Lamb arrives on the scene. It's him! The Lamb is worthy, and how I want to meet him face-to-face! How I want to see his glory!

And why is he worthy? Why is he glorious? It makes no sense—and it makes all the sense in God's great universe. It is because he was slain. It is because by his blood, in laying down his life, he ransomed people for God from every tribe and language and people and nation. That's why, according to this passage, Jesus is worthy to receive power and wealth and wisdom and might and honor and glory and blessing.

The glory of the slain Lamb—this is the ultimate glory, to which all other glory on earth and in heaven is only derivative. He makes his redeemed people into priests who reign, yes, but the glory bestowed on us flows from him, through him, and back to him again.

We're not receptacles for this blessed glory. We're conduits. The glory that has entered us came through the direct pouring motion of the Father, and the pour is supposed to continue. The pour of glory is designed to curve away from us in an arc, seeking once again to rejoin its source. We look like Light, we yearn for Light, and one day we rejoin Light. In the meantime, we whisper Light.

Light itself is a person who once walked the earth in man's clothes. He is the only One who is worthy to open the scroll.

Discussion Questions

- Who are the people in your life whose opinions matter the most to you? Who are you most eager for approval from?

- What are the things about yourself that you are most ashamed of—that you know will have to be transformed in order for you to stand comfortably in the new heaven and new earth?

- Have you ever spent time imagining the moment when you will stand before the Eyes That Matter? Spend time thinking about this. Imagine sights, sounds, and emotions. Meditate on 1 John 2:28 and 2 Cor. 5:10, which describe this moment.

- If you want a beautiful rendering of the end times through the eyes of C.S. Lewis, read the essay "The Weight of Glory," and the last chapter or two of both *The Last Battle (Chronicles of Narnia)* and *Till We Have Faces*. This will give you more fuel for your thought.

The Glory You Will Wear Forever

It is a serious thing to live in a society of possible gods and goddesses, to remember that the dullest and most uninteresting person you can talk to may one day be a creature which, if you saw it now, you would be strongly tempted to worship, or else a horror and corruption such as you now meet, if at all, only in a nightmare.

C.S. LEWIS, *The Weight of Glory*

The glories that we've looked at in this book have all been glories that any human being could possess. They are common graces—glories that any son or daughter of Adam could wear as part of our inheritance from God.

All these things were given to the human race as a whole, and we enjoy them, as we enjoy fresh air and sunshine. These common glories include our physical attributes, our possessions, and our abilities to think and to produce and to create and to relate. They can be witnessed by almost anyone who cares to look, and they are meant—like all of God's creation—to bring echoes of glory to his name.

But there is another kind of glory that is not visible to the naked (read: fallen) eye and are not common to the race as a whole. This is the glory that has been promised uniquely to those born in the *second* Adam, those who have been adopted as sons of God through Christ.

It is a glory that belongs, in large part, to the future:

> Though our outer self is wasting away, our inner self is being renewed day by day. For this light momentary affliction is preparing for us an eternal weight of glory beyond all comparison, as we look not to the things that are seen but to the things that are unseen. For the things that are seen are transient, but the things that are unseen are eternal (2 Corinthians 4:16-18).

Clearly this passage is contrasting an outer, seen, transient reality with an inner, unseen, eternal reality. Your body, your possessions, and even your mind and your talents may be fleeting—dying a natural death or being forcibly taken from you—but you have an inner self, too, and your inner self is being renewed. Afflictions are momentary, and they are in fact leading you directly into a future glory that can't be compared to anything you currently understand.

Paul waved the same prize (what John Piper calls "future glory") and beckoned us to run for it. He wrote, "To those who by patience in well-doing seek for glory and honor and immortality," he said, "he will give eternal life; but for those who are self-seeking, and do not obey the truth, but obey unrighteousness, there will be wrath and fury" (Romans 2:7-8).

What an odd way of putting it. There are two camps of people that Paul was contrasting: those who "by patience in well-doing seek for glory and honor and immortality" and those who "are self-seeking, and do not obey the truth."

Wait a second. Doesn't the first group sound like the second? How is it *not* self-seeking to seek for glory and honor? What is this self-seeking that the second group is guilty of, and how is it different from the first group?

It is clear from this passage that there is a right way and a wrong way to seek good for yourself. One way is commanded in Scripture—fighting for faith and obedience, looking to your reward. The other way is forbidden in Scripture—disobediently grasping for your desires in whatever way you see fit. One of these ways is motivated by a desire for reward from the Eyes That Matter. The other way is motivated by a desire for rewards of any kind, in any place, at any time, so long as the hunger can be staved off a bit longer.

In the end, this becomes a matter of choosing between smaller pleasures or greater pleasures. There are glorious and eternal rewards to be chosen over small and temporary ones.

C.S. Lewis puts it this way in *The Weight of Glory:*

> If we consider the unblushing promises of reward and the staggering nature of the rewards promised in the Gospels, it would seem that Our Lord finds our desires not too strong, but too weak. We are half-hearted creatures, fooling about with drink and sex and ambition when infinite joy is offered us, like an ignorant child who wants to go on making mud pies in a slum because he cannot imagine what is meant by the offer of a holiday at the sea. We are far too easily pleased.[1]

This means that when we cast our eyes on the pleasure of besting the glories around us, cultivating our ambition until we become unfit to look comfortably even on the glories of our fellow man, we are aiming too low. Envy is content to chase what cannot last and will not satisfy. Far from trying to prepare herself to stand before the Eyes That Matter, the envious woman is concerned only that she be able to stand before other women and not be outshined by any of them.

Envy means that we are, to turn Jim Elliot's phrase on its head, giving what we cannot lose in order to gain what we cannot keep. We are casting our eyes on the glory that comes from man because we are not remembering the glory that comes from God (John 12:43).

Four New Glories

In addition to the continuation and perfection of the borrowed glories we possess in this age, we'll have new glories in the age to come. These glories will be gifted to us permanently, and they will be the reason that our other glories can be worn without giving pain to ourselves or others.

1. Being Able to Gaze at God's Glory Unscathed and Worship It

Remember the terror and unapproachability of God that was experienced by the Jewish people:

> Mount Sinai was wrapped in smoke because the LORD had descended on it in fire. The smoke of it went up like the smoke of a kiln, and the whole mountain trembled greatly. And as the sound of the trumpet grew louder and louder, Moses spoke, and God answered him in thunder…And the LORD said to him, "Go down, and come up bringing Aaron with you. But do not let the priests and the people break through to come up to the LORD lest he break out against them" (Exodus 19:18-19,24).

These were the people whom God had reached out to in communication and adoption. They were his people, and he had made himself their ally—but still there was a great and necessary separation between them. Later, God talked with Moses "as a man speaks to his friend" (Exodus 33:11). Still, Moses had never seen God's face per se, because there is another scene when Moses asked for this privilege and a compromise was reached; he was allowed to look at God's back after God passed by. So apparently when Moses spoke to God as a man speaks to his friend, he still wasn't looking God full in the face, because no man could do that and live (Exodus 33:20).

Contrast this danger and separation with the way Adam and Eve were able to interact with God before the Fall, walking with him in the garden. Now contrast it with the way we will stand in God's presence at the close of this age.

In fact, part of our purpose—part of the reason we were born once, and then born a second time—was to witness the glory of the Father and the Son.

"Father," said Jesus in his High Priestly Prayer of John 17:24, "I desire that they also, whom you have given me, may be with me where I am, to see my glory that you have given me because you loved me before the foundation of the world." The people that he was about to purchase with his own body—he made it clear in his prayer what they were ultimately being purchased for. To be with him. To see his glory.

This is our eternal purpose. We will be able to look on his glory. We'll be able to stand it. We'll be uniquely outfitted to witness it and strong enough to enjoy it. We'll be fully transformed into glory conduits, able to withstand, absorb, and return the glory to its Source again in worship. God's intention for us has always been a kind of audience participation, in which he makes known "the riches of his glory for vessels of mercy, which he has prepared beforehand for glory" (Romans 9:23).

2. Being Like Christ and Sinless

Our joy would be far from complete if Christ did not make us like himself, perfect as our Father is perfect, as our Brother is perfect.

Without sin, our enjoyment of all God's good gifts will be untainted. We'll know love; we'll know joy; we'll know peace, patience, kindness, faithfulness, gentleness, and self-control. All our jokes will be funnier; all our work will be purposeful and enjoy-able; everything that we want, we will have, and everything that we have, we will want. We will always say all that ought to be said and never say what ought not to be said. We will still be creatures, living in God's world, under his rule, but we will have fulfilled our pur-pose utterly, finally. We will be a utopian community more perfect than any dreamed up by a cult leader. All the lions in our hearts will be swift to lie down with the lambs in the hearts of those around us. We will be tame, and stronger than ever.

I know these things to be true because I know that Jesus Christ our Brother was all these things even when he walked the earth. He did everything he ought, and he did not do anything he ought not. He said all and left nothing unsaid that was commanded him by the Father. He lived in lockstep with the Father's will and communed constantly in the Father's love—with the exception of those final moments on the cross, when he experienced total alienation from that same Father.

Our Lord was obedient. His glory was his obedience. And we will be like him, made after him in his image, finally imaging him in our completion. This process has begun even now: "We all, with unveiled face, beholding the glory of the Lord, are being trans-formed into the same image from one degree of glory to another. For this comes from the Lord who is the Spirit" (2 Corinthians 3:18).

3. Being Lavished with Eternal Wealth

Jesus several times talked about the kingdom of heaven in terms of investment of "talents," or coins. After all the glories we've exam-ined in this book, we can't help but look at the word "talent" a little more richly. Bodies, possessions, strengths, abilities, and spiritual gifts can all be looked at as talents, as a kind of earthly capital—and people are held responsible for our use of all of them.

Unblushingly, Jesus tells us to use these talents to earn reward points. He teases us with reward, to motivate good works such as being kind to your enemy as well as to your friend, and giving in secret rather than in the open. He tells us to lay up treasure in heaven in this way (Matthew 5:46; 6:1-21; 10:41-42).

For those who are faithful in a little, more is entrusted to them, Jesus said (Matthew 25:14-30). The dimmer, temporary gifts that God let us borrow in the previous age will give way to brighter and more permanent ones. And there is some sense, according to Scripture, in which we'll be rewarded in proportion to our deeds on earth.

Listen to the way that Paul put it:

> No one can lay a foundation other than that which is laid, which is Jesus Christ. Now if anyone builds on the foundation with gold, silver, precious stones, wood, hay, straw—each one's work will become manifest, for the Day will disclose it, because it will be revealed by fire, and the fire will test what sort of work each one has done. If the work that anyone has built on the foundation survives, he will receive a reward. If anyone's work is burned up, he will suffer loss, though he himself will be saved, but only as through fire (1 Corinthians 3:11-15).

This means more inequality.

Thanks to what we just talked about—the fact that we'll be sinless like our Lord—these inequalities won't bring us pain and dissatisfaction. But it is clear that Paul wanted us to look at this prospect of having our works tested by fire, with a reward at the end of the test, and be motivated to good works. To put it crudely, he wanted us to see that heaven is not a pass/fail proposition—not entirely. It is a situation in which all who have believed in Jesus are declared righteous and welcomed into the presence of the Father. But it is also apparently a situation in which our work on earth is examined, and there is a *reward based on that examination.*

However this shakes out in reality, we will see ourselves richer than we've ever dreamed in the new heaven and new earth, that much is a fact. The imagery used in Scripture to describe heaven is full of precious stones, crowns, thrones, mansions, rivers, and cities. Jesus told his followers, "In my Father's house are many rooms. If it were not so, would I have told you that I go to prepare a place for you? And if I go and prepare a place for you, I will come again and will take you to myself, that where I am you may be also" (John 14:2-3).

These promises give hope, because it is clear that whatever the images mean, they mean plenty, and comfort, and joy, and pleasures forevermore.

And they are meant to motivate us. As Paul wrote to the Corinthians, "Do you not know that in a race all the runners run, but only one gets the prize? Run in such a way as to get the prize. Everyone who competes in the games goes into strict training. They do it to get a crown that will not last; but we do it to get a crown that will last forever" (1 Corinthians 9:24-25 NIV).

4. Being in Authority over Creation

Who are the sorts of people that wear crowns? Kings. Kings wear crowns.

Apparently Jesus has prepared jobs for us in the new heaven and new earth, and these jobs involve authority. Revelation 22 tells us that in that day, the servants of God will live in his presence and under his light without terror, witnessing the glory of the Lamb and having the Lamb's name on their foreheads. There is a constant renewal of health and prosperity, with an absence of futility. And even with the throne of God and the Lamb in the midst of them, these servants will in some way reign forever and ever.

This is the wish of anyone who is in authority over anything, no matter how small. We want a prosperous reign, tenure, party committee, or whatever it is we're supposed to be in charge of. We want unabated peace, health, and prosperity. Apparently, the new heaven and new earth will provide all these things for all eternity, and we are going to be kings and queens over these domains.

Other passages use the word "priests" to describe the saints in the new heaven and new earth, and from this we better understand the worshipful nature of our jobs in heaven. Our jobs will be that of chief worshippers, every one of us. This is the reason we were given the crowns of glory in the first place—only to play a part in the court of the High King. The court should be full of glittering courtiers. But their rich robes are only there to bring texture and ceremony to the High King's reign. Their voices are only given them to be raised in songs and shouts of praise. The court must be peopled. And Christ the Lamb has peopled it:

> By your blood you ransomed people for God
>   from every tribe and language and people and nation,
> and you have made them a kingdom and priests to our God,
>   and they shall reign on the earth (Revelation 5:9-10).

Jesus promised his 12 apostles special places of authority, judging the 12 tribes of Israel. In the same breath, he talked about some related reward for everyone who forsakes other things for his name:

> Truly, I say to you, in the new world, when the Son of Man will sit on his glorious throne, you who have followed me will also sit on twelve thrones, judging the twelve tribes of Israel. And everyone who has left houses or brothers or sisters or father or mother or children or lands, for my name's sake, will receive a hundredfold and will inherit eternal life (Matthew 19:28-29).

Paul pointed out that just as death reigned because of the one man Adam's trespass, God's people will reign in life through the one man Jesus Christ (Romans 5:17). We'll take dominion over the new earth as we were never able to fully do in the previous age.

So Back to the Envy

There will be no envy in heaven.

There will be envy in hell.

There will be inequalities in both places.

Heaven will contain inequalities. But in a sinless state, human beings will know themselves, know their God, and know each other. They will have a right regard for the glories of the Father, of the Son, and of the Holy Spirit. They will have a lesser but proper regard for the glories they and other created beings—such as angels, and their fellow man—have been gifted with. Envy, like other sin, has no place in heaven. Perfected men do not envy. They worship.

Hell will also contain inequalities. We're assured by some of the language used in the New Testament that it will be "more tolerable" for some than for others in the outer darkness (Matthew 11:24). Where there is inequality, misery, and hatred, there is envy. Besides this, the greatest part of the envy practiced by Satan and his followers will be reserved for those whom they know to be in the kingdom of the Father. They will be locked into this circle of hatred endlessly, grinding their teeth in the torment of the outcast.

Prepare yourself to be a citizen of whichever kingdom you choose. You will play by its rules forever.

You can even now begin to gain victory over envy, as you look forward to the joy set before you. This age of painful inequality can be more like the next one of joyful inequality. Because the further up and the further in (C.S. Lewis) you go, the more enveloped in the glorious light of God's grace, you will find that the inequalities feel less and less significant.

How can you begrudge the difference between an eternally happy baker and an eternally gleeful cupbearer? They're both living in joy and serving the king. How can you look at the hairline difference between one eternity of bliss and another eternity of bliss in a slightly different color? How can you find the heart to quibble over the difference between having been forgiven a death-sentence worth of sin and having been forgiven a death-sentence worth of different sin? The more you see your own position through God's eyes, and the better you understand the outrageous overflow of good things coming your way in the presence of the Eyes That Matter, the less possible it will be to mutter to yourself over your friend's husband's new job.

It's simply impossible to look fully on the promises of God for this age and the next without finding hope and solace in the face of inequality. Pray, and you will have help. Arm yourself properly against the flesh and the devil, and you will be victorious. Love and study God's Word, and you will find yourself equipped.

And give thanks. Let us learn to sing this song now. It's a song we will sing throughout eternity along with the psalmist:

> You have turned for me my mourning into dancing;
>   you have loosed my sackcloth
>   and clothed me with gladness,
> that my glory may sing your praise and not be silent.
>   O Lord my God, I will give thanks to you forever!
>   (Psalm 30:11-12).

Discussion Questions

- Some of the glories we can expect to wear for all eternity include "being able to gaze at God's glory unscathed and worship it," "being like Christ and sinless," "being eternally rich with some kind of reward," and "being in authority over creation." After reading this chapter, which of these new, future glories is the most immediately exciting to you?

- Which of these promises will come in most handy to you personally when dealing with the inequalities and disappointments of our fallen world?

- Having finished this book about envy and the glory of God, what are some takeaways you came away with? What do you plan to do tomorrow to fight the sin of envy in your life?

Happiness Is the Best Revenge?

The Lord is so gracious to me.

There are some things in your heart that almost undo you when you find out about them. When I was first convicted of envy, it had been a staple of my existence for at least 20 years. The process of beginning this book came directly out of the first round of repentance and reconciliation. Then there were a few years when I set the project aside. I needed to feel my way forward to see what would become of the damaged relationships in real life.

Can a Christian bounce back from this kind of sin? I wondered. *Can these relationships ever be the same?*

All I can say—again—is that the Lord is gracious beyond measure to me. Conviction of sin is a sweet gift that belongs to the children of God; it's a luxury that the lost don't know. Repentance is another luxury. True and lasting reconciliation is another.

The desire to know and love my sisters came first. The means to do so came next. The willingness on their end was there all along. If you had told me seven years ago that I was going to develop a reflexive reaction of joy when I heard about good things happening to my sisters—all four of them, in fact—I would have looked at the ground in shame and disbelief. But this is the truth. They are my friends.

Toward other friends I must use a touchstone on my heart continually to see what it's full of.

Just in the last few weeks—right in the middle of polishing this manuscript—I had to confess another instance of rooted envy toward a newer friend. It's been years since I had to do this. Because it was a new glory that I hadn't envied before, it took longer for me to repent than it should have. She instantly and graciously forgave.

Then she told me that she was currently struggling with envy toward another unnamed person, and we rejoiced together that our conversation had opened an opportunity for her to examine her heart and approach another friend. And this is how sweet the Lord is. He will sometimes even set up chain reactions of repentance and grace for us.

The words of Psalm 51 paint such an accurate picture of the painful and glorious process that God keeps putting my heart through:

> Have mercy on me, O God,
>   according to your steadfast love;
>   according to your abundant mercy
>   blot out my transgressions.
> Wash me thoroughly from my iniquity,
>   and cleanse me from my sin!…
>
> Against you, you only, have I sinned
>   and done what is evil in your sight,
>   so that you may be justified in your words
>   and blameless in your judgment…
>
> Purge me with hyssop, and I shall be clean;
>   wash me, and I shall be whiter than snow.

Let me hear joy and gladness;
> let the bones that you have broken rejoice…

Create in me a clean heart, O God,
> and renew a right spirit within me.

Cast me not away from your presence,
> and take not your Holy Spirit from me.

Restore to me the joy of your salvation,
> and uphold me with a willing spirit.

Then I will teach transgressors your ways,
> and sinners will return to you.

Deliver me from bloodguiltiness, O God,
> O God of my salvation,
> and my tongue will sing aloud of your righteousness.

O Lord, open my lips,
> and my mouth will declare your praise.

For you will not delight in sacrifice, or I would give it;
> you will not be pleased with a burnt offering.

The sacrifices of God are a broken spirit;
> a broken and contrite heart, O God, you will
> not despise (Psalm 51:1-2,4,7-17).

People say that happiness is the best revenge. "Be happy," says the world, "because it makes your enemies crazy."

Christ takes this kind of wisdom and twists it until it is hope instead of hatred. If you find yourself wanting revenge on your (perhaps imagined) enemies, then the only thing to do is to turn and drink deeply of Christ himself. To this hour, it is the most viscerally effective thing for me when I see myself turning up a crop of resentment and insecurity.

Christ—his nature, his great act of love for you, his promises of glory, his beauty, his living word, and the fact that you'll see his face soon—is the happiness you must seek. If you desire revenge on your enemies, then turn and drink from this fountain. You will get your revenge in a way you never expected. Christ will be your happiness, and it will be such happiness that revenge itself will be killed.

That is when enemies become friends, friends become blood sisters, and blood sisters—indeed—become friends.

Notes

Chapter 1: What Is Glory? And What Does Envy Have to Do with It?

1. Douglas Moo, *Romans* (Grand Rapids, MI: Eerdmans, 1996), 108.

2. John Milton, *Paradise Lost*, bk. 1, lines 106-111, 115-16; http://www.bartleby.com/4/401.html.

3. Ibid., bk. 1, line 263.

4. Ibid., bk. 2, lines 358-69; http://www.bartleby.com/4/402.html.

Chapter 2: The Unbearable Inequality: Understanding Envy

1. William Shakespeare, *Anthony and Cleopatra*, Act 3, Scene 1.

2. Shakespeare, *Othello*, Act 3, Scene 3.

3. William L. Davidson, "Envy and Emulation," in James Hastings, ed., *Encyclopedia of Religion and Ethics*, vol. 5. (New York: Scribner/Clark, 1912).

4. Aristotle, *Rhetoric*, Book II, ch. 9.

5. Thomas Aquinas, *Summa Theologica*, II-II. Q. 36. Art. 1, Translated by Fathers of the English Dominican Province (Coyote Canyon Press, Kindle Edition, 2010).

6. Augustine (edited by Loren Gavitt), *Saint Augustine's Prayer Book* (n.p.: Holy Cross Publications, 1947).

7. Jonathan Edwards, *Ethical Writings*, in Paul Ramsey, ed., *The Works of Jonathan Edwards*, vol. 8 (New Haven, Connecticut: Yale University Press, 1989), 219.

8. F. F. Bruce, *The Epistle to the Galatians: A Commentary on the Greek Text* (Grand Rapids, MI: Eerdmans, 1982), 249.

9. Frederick Buechner, *Wishful Thinking: A Seeker's ABC* (San Francisco: HarperOne, 1993), 24.

10. Joe Rigney, "Envy" in *Killjoys*, Marshall Segal, ed. (Desiring God, Kindle Edition, 2015), location 415.

11. There's one Greek word that is pretty much always translated as envy—and it's always used in a bad sense. That word is *phthonos*, and it's the word used in all the passages we looked at except one. But there's another Greek word for jealous, *zelos*, that can be both positive and negative. In a good sense, it can mean zeal. In its negative sense, it's sometimes translated as *envy*, sometimes as *jealousy*. In those verses, the meanings of *envy* and *jealousy* are almost synonymous.

12. C.S. Lewis, "Screwtape Proposes a Toast" from *The World's Last Night* (reprinted with permission by The Macmillan Company, New York, 1959), 174-75; italics in original.

Chapter 4: Borrowed Magnets: The Envy of Charm and Influence

1. Paul Tripp, "It's Not Your Party," January 29, 2014, https://www.paultripp.com/wednesdays-word/posts/its-not-your-party.

Chapter 6: Borrowed Money: The Envy of Options

1. Helmut Schoeck, *Envy: A Theory of Social Behavior* (New York: Harcourt, Brace & World, 1969).
2. Randy Alcorn, *The Treasure Principle* (Sisters, OR: Multnomah, 2005), 50-51.

Chapter 7: Borrowed Art: The Envy of Creativity

1. Peter Shaffer, screenwriter, *Amadeus* (film), 1984.
2. Shaffer.
3. Shaffer.
4. Shaffer.
5. New World Encyclopedia contributors, "Johannes Kepler," *New World Encyclopedia,* http://www.newworldencyclopedia.org/p/index.php?title=Johannes_Kepler&oldid=982321 (accessed February 2, 2018).

Chapter 11: The Eyes That Matter: Why We Need God's Approval After All

1. Yes, that's a real place, and that's the real name of their elementary school.
2. C.S. Lewis, *Till We Have Faces* (New York, New York: Harcourt, Inc., 1956), 110-11; emphasis in original.
3. Lewis, *Till We Have Faces,* 172-73.
4. C.S. Lewis, "The Weight of Glory," in *The Weight of Glory and Other Addresses* (New York: HarperCollins, 1949), 38-39.

Chapter 12: The Glory You Will Wear Forever

1. Lewis, *The Weight of Glory,* 26.

Acknowledgments

A woman flashed me in my own office once.

It was during a scheduled interview on a Saturday. The newspaper where I worked at the time always did a special ad section for Breast Cancer Awareness Month, and we always interviewed a survivor.

This time the subject was a woman in her 70s whom I'd never met. She told me an incredible story about how her cancer was found, eliminated, found again, cut out (with every penny of the $77,000 bill covered by insurance she signed up for two hours before the surgery), and probably (but not necessarily) gone for good.

Her hair was dyed an implausible red, her manner brisk and matter-of-fact. She told me her story with the delighted attitude of any raconteur who has discovered a story in her own life that people like to hear.

"Wanna see?" she said then.

"No, thank you," I would have said, except there was no time.

She lifted her shirt up, no bra, and showed me those scars, along with everything else.

I've always been a little squeamish about random acts of nudity and anything that even suggests itself as a wound. But it seemed rude to run screaming from my own office. So as she flashed me her scars and skin, I just nodded politely and *hmmed*.

I bring up this story because it reminds me of the way some of the stories in this book might come across. It can be a bit like the survivor-gone-wild display in my office that day: probably too much information, ugly and personal, shared with total strangers.

And when I sit down to thank the people who made it possible for this book to move forward, I think first of the handful who gave me permission to use stories in which I envy them. The stories are only unflattering to one person (me), but they still involve others who were each so very gracious that they didn't hesitate for a second about having the stories shared. So I have to thank my sisters (Sophie, Callie, and Phoebe were all referenced) and then a few unnamed friends whose identities are protected by name changes. You know who you are.

I also have to thank my husband, who did much more than your average supportive reading in the development of this book. Here's what happened. When I began it, he agreed to help me by cowriting it and being the theologically precise voice to my narrative one. When it became clear that this structure for the project wasn't working, he gave me his full blessing to run forward into the material, but not before I had fistfuls of passages in hand that were his own writing, not mine. They were integrated into the final version so seamlessly that I can no longer tell where his voice ends and mine begins (a little bit like marriage itself). This attitude of freehanded humility is characteristic of Justin Dillehay. I love you, darling.

I have to thank my father, who was the first person to tell me I should write, and—perhaps more importantly—the person who sat me on his lap and taught me to read. His is still the stamp of approval that I require to know something is good. And I am thankful to my mother, who always shares these things on Facebook and who is no literary schlump herself.

Thank you to my agent, Bruce Barbour, without whom I would still be a dreaming unpublished author.

Thank you to the team at Harvest House, who have made it clear that they are a hardworking family band. Especially my editor, Kathleen Kerr, whose sharp eye and rampant enthusiasm has made me feel like her favorite compliment, a "rock star."

Other assorted people supported the book by reading some or all and offering feedback, some long before it was published: Rachael Holliday, Chris and Tiffany Davis, Maria Hollingsworth, Ashley Busby, Ivan Mesa, Caroline Newheiser, and a group of women at Grace Baptist Hartsville who did a book study on this book and encouraged me when I needed a little push—most especially Jane Martin, head cheerleader; Julie Clement, who talked a lot (in a good way); and Juanita Pinzur, who helped me to see that I use too many commas.

Thank you all!

"I thank my God in all my remembrance of you, always in every prayer of mine for you all making my prayer with joy, because of your partnership in the gospel from the first day until now" (Philippians 1:3-5).

About the Author

Tilly Dillehay holds a degree in journalism from Lipscomb University. In the past, she has been the editor of a weekly newspaper and of a lifestyle magazine, and she now serves as homemaker and mother to two little girls. She writes at www.justinandtilly.com and contributes occasionally to The Gospel Coalition. She is the host of *The Green Workshop*, an event for women on the subject of envy that is held in local churches. Tilly's husband, Justin, is a pastor in the small town east of Nashville where the family resides.

To learn more about Harvest House books and
to read sample chapters, visit our website:

www.harvesthousepublishers.com

HARVEST HOUSE PUBLISHERS
EUGENE, OREGON